China's New Culture of Cool

Understanding the world's fastest-growing market

Lianne Yu

Cynthia Chan

Christopher Ireland

New Riders

VOICES THAT MATTER™

China's New Culture of Cool: Understanding the world's fastest-growing market
Lianne Yu, Cynthia Chan, and Christopher Ireland

New Riders
1249 Eighth Street
Berkeley, CA 94710
510/524-2178, 800/283-9444
510/524-2221 (fax)

Find us on the Web at: www.newriders.com
To report errors, please send a note to errata@peachpit.com

New Riders is an imprint of Peachpit, a division of Pearson Education

Interior Design: Ralph Fowler
Composition: WolfsonDesign

ISBN 0-321-45344-1

9 8 7 6 5 4 3 2 1

Printed and bound in the United States of America

Advance Praise for China's New Culture of Cool

First and foremost, this is a book about people: the young adults of China. Told with great insight and deep affection for China, this is a must-read, easy-to-understand book for both business and pleasure travel to a fascinating country. Drawing on their social science backgrounds, decades of studying people around the globe, and ten years of study of this extraordinary and changing place, the authors bring to life the people, the culture, the traditions, and changes. If you have time to read only one book before going, this is the one to choose.

—*Carolyn Fuson, Sr. Research Manager, Windows Live, Microsoft Corporation*

For those who seek out sensible orientation and extensive updates on China's consumers insights—read it! You will get to know what China's young consumers consider "cool" within their own cultural context and unique lifestyles. This is a very intuitive book that increases our insight into the fast-emerging and ever-transforming China market.

—*Ben Tsiang, Co-Founder & Executive VP, SINA (China's largest web portal)*

This is a guidebook that will clarify navigating this exciting journey through China's culture of cool created by its youth. It is a perfect read for those desiring an understanding of the effects the enormous change has brought to China throughout the last decade, as seen through their perspective. Technology, food, fashion are the areas that provide global inspiration for innovation and imagination. A necessary read.

—*Richard Saul Wurman, Creator of the TED and eg Conferences*

Having seen the Chinese consumer revolution unfold in front of my eyes for the last 10 years, I find this book a must-read for any marketer committed to understanding the Chinese consumer experience.

—*Bernd Schmitt, Author, Customer Experience Management*

The future is created by the young, and *China's New Culture of Cool* is our first real portal into the mindset of China's young people today and their impact on the emerging China economy of tomorrow.

—*Moira Gunn, Host, Tech Nation on NPR Talk*

Clear, direct and insightful commentary about the seismic market shift that's occurring on the other side of the planet. An invaluable resource!

—*Clement Mok, Director of Global Design Planning/Sapient*

This book paints a vivid picture of how the young and entrepreneurial in China are driving change in its cities. Reading it is the next best thing to going there and experiencing it yourself.

—*Jon Jerde, FAIA, Founder and Chairman, The Jerde Partnership*

Hurry and read *China's New Culture of Cool*. My wife and I signed the first shoe contract with China in 1974. Now over 80 percent of all shoes sold in the U.S. are made in China. Along with that statistic, there are millions more cell phones in China than people in the U.S. These inspiring insights show how youth can change the way we all live, as we seek our own future.

—*Cabell Brand, Chairman, Cabell Brand Center for International Poverty and Resource Studies*

Contents

Chapter 5
Yi (style)

Chapter 6
Shi (food)

Chapter 7
Zhu (living)

Chapter 8
Xing (mobility)

Chapter 9
Future Present

Acknowledgements

Many thanks to my co-authors for an amazing experience and to my colleagues at Cheskin, who supported us during the writing of this book by staunchly defending our right to a good work-life balance. I am especially grateful to Katherine Lee for her gorgeous photos and insights into youth culture, and to Tony Senna for his willingness to tackle anything new. Shirley Yang and everyone at Hyperlink made my research in China feel nearly effortless. Thanks to my family, who never quite know what I'm up to but support me wholeheartedly; to Mel, fellow *huaqiao* and grungy backpacker across China; and to Heiko, for taking me scuba diving whenever I needed a break. During my 1990-1991 stay at Beijing University, I was fortunate to meet many remarkable Chinese students and teachers who generously welcomed me into their lives. I dedicate this book to them.

—LiAnne Yu

Painting is one of the four traditional arts in Chinese culture, and as I worked with my co-authors, LiAnne and Christopher, numerous other people supported me in painting this memorable piece. My heartfelt thanks go to my Cheskin colleagues, especially Katherine Lee and Tony Senna, whose many stories from their China trips added richness and detail to our content. I also want to acknowledge my longtime friends Agnes Ip, Cynthia Lam, Susan Wong, and Michael Dundas for their generosity in sharing their insights about China, introducing me to their friends, and giving me firsthand exposure to the emerging, rapidly changing culture of cool in China. Additional thanks to my friends at Consumer Search in China, who tolerated my endless requests for photos, interviews, and information while writing this book. And how could I not thank my family, who placed full confidence and support in my storytelling endeavor? A huge *xie xie* to everyone on my *guanxi* list!

—Cynthia Chan

This book has been a joy to write, mainly due to my remarkable co-authors, LiAnne Yu and Cynthia Chan, who seemed to be available to collaborate at all hours of the day or night. An equally remarkable resource was Terri Ducay, who agonized over the quality and placement of every single photograph in this book and improved images taken from racing taxi cabs, in poor light, or after one too many Tsingtao beers. Without her experienced eye and saintly patience, this would book would have jagged edges. I also wish to acknowledge the generosity of my colleagues at Cheskin who excused me from normal day-to-day tasks as I worked on this book. And last but certainly not least, the good-humored tolerance of my family, who asked me to please write the next book from someplace other than our living room.

—Christopher Ireland

Finally, the authors would like to thank Denise Klarquist, Pam Paradiso, and Etienne Fang for their support at various stages of the creation of this book; Cheskin's principals, Davis Masten and Darrel Rhea, for their support of this project; and our editor, Marjorie Baer, and everyone at Peachpit/New Riders who helped bring this book to life.

Introduction

The youth population in any country fascinates us. The newness of their perspective, the innocence of their exploration, and the sheer joy of their playfulness is a powerful tonic when life seems overly defined and predictable. But we are particularly drawn to this current generation of young Chinese, because they embody all of these characteristics and in addition some that are rarely seen elsewhere. These young people, roughly 15 to 29 years of age, are contributing significantly to the economic growth and cultural development of China. They are fearless in their pursuit of the "good life," confident of a future that will be better than the past or present. They are a generation of early adopters, happily leaving behind a less colorful past and embracing all that business, technology, and commerce promise to deliver. In comparison to their more skeptical and jaded peers in more developed countries, China's teens and young adults are refreshingly idealistic, optimistic, and happy.

China's 1.3 billion people are all important to understand, but it is the 200 million young people—specifically those living in the country's dozen or so major urban cities—who are experiencing the most change in their lives and who are leading much of it as well. It is these young trendsetters who we follow and profile in this book. As a further point of definition, this book highlights four key areas of young people's lives that we believe are undergoing the most change: food, style, living and mobility. Each individual section discusses what change is happening, why it's happening, and how young China is responding. It's not meant as a quick "top trends" list, but rather as an illustration that helps readers understand what it means to be a young Chinese urbanite in 2006.

We write this book from the perspective of ethnographers, researchers, and business people who have a connection to China and its youthful population. LiAnne Yu, an American of Chinese decent, first visited Beijing as an exchange student in 1990. She immediately felt welcomed by her new teachers and fellow Chinese students as a "huaqiao," or overseas Chinese. But for LiAnne, China was much different from the ancestral homeland of her childhood imagination. There were no kung fu fighters or women dressed in colorful Qing dynasty outfits fanning themselves while being pulled around in rickshaws. Rather, she found a country that had just been through an incredible amount of political turbulence and was then in the midst of economic change.

As a young adult in China in the 1990s, LiAnne noticed that only the very elite and wealthy Chinese and expatriates could enjoy leisure-time activities such as bowling at the New World Hotel, shopping at the first "modern" mall, the Friendship Store, dancing at the Lido disco, or enjoying the all-you-can-eat buffet spreads at the upscale hotels. In fact, she recalls that only foreign passport holders were allowed. She was shocked to find that for the average Chinese, the KFC that had recently opened near Tiananmen was a significant indulgence, something they saved up to enjoy. She also remembers everyday shopping as dreary at best. The salespeople were almost universally cranky, but over time LiAnne came to see this unpleasantness not as a reflection of their personalities, but rather as a natural result of the state-run economy. No one had any financial incentive to work hard, or to work at all. Gossiping with other state-employed shopkeepers was more fun and rewarding than waiting on customers.

Looking back, LiAnne marvels over how much China has changed in the past 15 years—not just in terms of the country's economy and physical surroundings, meaning the whole environment—buildings, signs merchandise, cars, marketplace, etc.—but also the attitudes of its people. In her early visits, people could easily identify LiAnne as Chinese American. Even if she spoke perfect "Putonghua" (Mandarin), one look at her clothes, her tan, the way she walked, her haircut, and they knew right away she was not from China and would treat her differently. Nowadays, it's easy for LiAnne to blend in with the mix of Asian nationalities that crowd China's urban streets. If she stands out now, it's because she's dressed less fashionably than the majority of young Chinese women she meets.

Cynthia Chan was born in Hong Kong, then a British colony, now (as of 1997) part of China. As she grew up during the 1980s and 1990s, Hong Kong's proximity to the mainland helped her feel close to China. But the vast differences in lifestyle and culture created aloofness. Cynthia's first impression of mainland China came from a family trip to Shenzhen in the southern region. She and her family stayed at a resort complex close to a theme park, but the long lines at immigration, unsanitary restrooms, concerns about the safety of water and food, and questionably safe rides all detracted from the experience. As for customer service? It was non-existent.

Fortunately that initial taste of China did not discourage Cynthia from learning more about the country, and as a young adult, she began traveling around China for both work and leisure. Repeated trips over the past ten years have moved Cynthia from a state of doubt and concern for China's future to a state of awe. She is convinced that someone has pushed an invisible fast-forward button; what else could explain the speed and extent of the changes she sees each time she returns? She is engrossed by the way the entire country—from the oldest government officials to the youngest children—now embraces the concept of development.

As Cynthia sees it, not only is China "fast-forwarding" the development of homes and businesses spread across its almost 6 million square miles, but it's also proactive. Through its products and its people, Chinese culture is traveling on ships, trains, trucks, and the Internet and joining the rest of the world—striving to be seen not as producers of low-quality goods or as people with substandard living conditions, but as equals to the successful nations of Japan, Korea, the U.S., and the European Union.

Christopher is the outlier in this trio. Her expertise is in understanding youth populations. Like most of the readers of this book, for most of her life her exposure to China has been secondhand. Although her grandmother was among the first tourists allowed into the country in the 1970s, unfortunately she did not take her granddaughter along. During Christopher's tenure at Cheskin, she has led hundreds of projects that included China as a market, but since she doesn't speak Cantonese or Mandarin, others were always more qualified to do the fieldwork there.

All that changed this past year when she boarded a 747 with hundreds of other China-bound passengers to begin a two-week stay that exposed her to an overwhelming range of people, places, and processes. She dined with families in their suburban apartments and played computer games with young singles in a hutong home. She rode the hair-raising Shanghai taxis from one end of the city to the other, visiting new restaurants, shopping centers both above and below ground, gigantic living complexes, start-up businesses, and neon-clad entertainment areas. She ate partridge eggs from a vendor's cart in Beijing, Peking Duck in a state-owned restaurant, and an assortment of vegetables, fruits, and meats she had never seen before, much less consumed.

From sun-up to well past sundown, her English-speaking guides answered every question she asked, spontaneously arranged interviews with people on the street, and asked random strangers if they would kindly let the American take their picture. From Christopher's perspective, China is a very capable, modern country presenting itself in a positive and hopeful manner. She's entranced by the nation's seemingly unlimited desire to innovate, and is firmly convinced that China will be the country to produce the flying car she's wanted since fourth grade.

We hope you find this book enjoyable and our observations insightful, but it is not a substitute for firsthand exposure. If you've traveled in China recently, our photos and comments may recall impressions you had while there. If you've not been there recently, now would be a good time to learn "hello" in Mandarin, *Ni hao*.

1

A Generation of
Early Adopters

When mainland China cautiously re-opened its borders to U.S. tourists in the 1970's, a small surge of curious travelers hastened to see the country whose leaders had hidden it from view for decades. Their questions reflected the concerns of most Americans at that time: Could over a billion people survive under a communist political and economic system? Was China's way of life an alternative to the democratic capitalism propelling growth and prosperity in the West? While rightfully impressed with the country's size and history, this first wave of visitors relayed somber stories that largely discredited the Mao regime. They told of masses barely making a living amidst dirty, aging buildings, and dilapidated roadways. They described cities crowded with people who seemed resigned to live an uninspiring life. The magnificent Great Wall and the glorious Forbidden Palace still stood as symbols of China's ancient dominance, but few saw any signs of more recent success. To most American visitors—whether tourists, journalists, or business travelers—carefully shepherded around on government-authorized tours, China's culture appeared frozen in time: a seemingly monolithic society dressed in identical gray jackets.

Press your TiVo button and fast-forward 30 years. The hundreds of planes that daily carry visitors to China from around the world have few if any empty seats. New luxury high-rise hotels line the streets of Beijing, Shanghai, Guangzhou, Xian, Chengdu and at

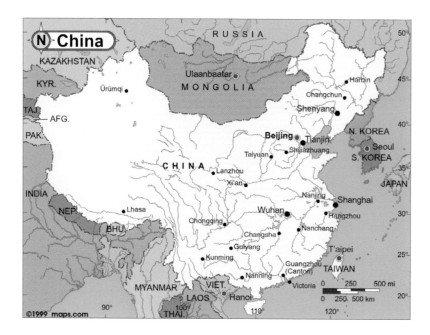

least a dozen other large urban centers. Well-designed restaurants teem with stylishly dressed Chinese patrons comparing new mobile phones or discussing travel plans. Young Chinese boys and girls wander cheerfully through massive malls imagining the riches their future holds. Millions of cars, motorcycles, and bicycles carry their ambitious passengers to work or school on newly paved streets, while thousands of miles of high-speed subways snake across the Eastern provinces in service of newly affluent suburbanites enjoying a dramatically improved standard of living. Although the rural sections of China still struggle with poverty and despair, most of the country's 1.3 billion citizens— particularly the 640 million who are under age 30—are optimistic about their future. For young Chinese men and women, "now" is the right time and China is the right place for them to begin living rich and colorful lives.

It's these young adults, particularly those whose incomes put them in China's growing middle class, who are the stars of this book. They are powerful influences both within China and throughout the world because of their massive buying power and their willingness to break traditions. They are the new consumers whom global brands are counting on for future growth. Their collective actions, which often explore new territory, are the leading edge of change in China's culture, its society and its citizens' day-to-day lives.

Revolutionary Change

How China transformed itself from a parent's admonition ("Eat your dinner! Children in China are starving!") to the world's poster child of rising commercial success in less than three decades is the topic of dozens of recently published books and too many college theses to count. Opinions vary from one expert to the next, and it will likely be decades more before a definitive explanation is widely accepted. In the meantime, as context for our look at the leading edge of market change in China, we offer a short course on the four primary moves that carried the country from a drab past to a vibrant future.

1. Moving from a centralized to a market-driven economy

Although many Westerners think of China as a strict and rigid society, this impression probably gives too much emphasis to the country's behavior in the 20th century, particularly during the long reign of Mao Zedong, who headed the government as Communist Party Chairman from 1949 until his death in 1976. Mao's leadership was the governmental equivalent of a tsunami. In reaction to centuries of an imperial society, his revolutionary administration overturned the hierarchy, wiped out private property, exiled the educated and elite to the hinterlands, and turned everyone into "comrades" in a sea of communes and state-owned enterprises.

In this planned society, Chinese consumers had few choices and little opportunity for individual expression through personal possessions. In fact, even the notion of consumerism was nonexistent, because in Mao's China, such acts were considered bourgeois and counter-revolutionary. The government further depressed the economy by nationalizing most companies, restaurants and retailers. With no financial incentive to improve their offerings, managers had no reason to compete.

Thirty years later, Mao's picture remains a larger-than-life icon towering over the Gate of Heavenly Peace across from Tiananmen Square, but his socialist doctrine is rapidly being remodeled to accommodate market-driven principles. China took the first steps toward loosening its socialist constraints and permitting commercial growth under Deng Xiao Ping, Mao's successor. Deng explained his bottom-line orientation and lack of reverence for a strict Communist ideology, "It does not matter whether the cat is white or black; if it catches mice, it is a good cat." That "good cat" was capitalism, and Deng reintroduced it into Chinese culture first by creating Special Economic Zones in the Southern provinces that attracted foreign investment and gave these regions a head start on growth and prosperity. In 2001, China sought admission to the World Trade Organization, and its entry into the WTO further opened its doors to the rest of the world.

Although many aspects of China's planned society remain in place and may never change, its current economy is best described as mixed "capitalism with Chinese characteristics." It is a hybrid of Western capitalism and Chinese socialism, in which the Communist Party retains political power but encourages

Young Chinese commuters glance at Mao's portrait on the Gate of Heavenly Peace as they rush off to work in a capitalist China the Chairman would not recognize.

a free market economy. At this point China operates under an almost fully capitalistic economy but still employs a one-party rule. In doing so, China is the first major world economy to successfully transition to a capitalist economy without even a semblance of a democratic political process in place. Its success signals to the rest of the world that democracy may not be the only road to riches.

In addition to capturing the attention of every political scientist on the planet, this new market orientation has spurred China's culturally inherent—but until recently, largely unexpressed—competitiveness. At the most macro level, its governmental leaders compete for world respect and lucrative trade pacts. When China's President Hu Jintao's stopped off at Microsoft in April of 2006 to meet with Bill Gates before visiting President Bush in Washington, he was not driven solely by the logistical convenience. He was also building a mutually beneficial partnership between Microsoft

Headlines and images proclaiming China's success call out from newsstands and bookstores throughout the country, regularly reminding its citizens of their new prominence and power.

and China. Among China's rising entrepreneurial class, business owners compete for opportunities and customers, hosting industry conferences weekly that are attended by avid investors and developers from every country. Chinese students, many of whom learn English as children, compete intensely for entrance into universities and later, for highly prized positions with multinational companies doing business in China. Even China's consumers, who have a long tradition of bargaining for the best deal, now use those skills to compete for the highest status luxury brands or the newest fashions from Korea.

The impact of the country's growing competitiveness registers with China's young urbanites every day. City newsstands and bookstores are filled with magazines heralding China's amazing economic prowess. The grocery shelves are bursting with brightly packaged imported and domestic products only available to populations who have advanced beyond the subsistence level. Visits from global and leaders are becoming more the rule than the exception.

Underlying all these visible signs of success is real growth. In fact, China's rapid economic and societal transformation would be breathtaking even if it were moving at half its current rate. Since 1980, the Chinese economy has grown by more than 9 percent a year. In terms of purchasing power, the country's economy is now second only to the U.S. Chinese citizens have enjoyed an equally rapid rise in their average income and personal wealth. From 1997 to 2004, China's average household income rose 30 percent to approximately 14,000 Yuan ($1,800 U.S., as tracked by China's National Bureau of Statistics). Although this still seems quite small by Western standards, if the U.S. experienced this rate of growth, our average annual household income would rise from $54,135 to $70,375. That would be a nice raise.

Granted, this newly earned wealth is not evenly distributed throughout the country. Those who have most benefited from China's economic reforms are overwhelmingly urban. The roughly 660 million people still living in rural areas do not share this modern lifestyle, and some percentage do not aspire to it. But the 50 million or more who annually migrate from the rural towns to the country's largest cities are chasing the market-driven dream and hoping they will be competitive enough and lucky enough to catch it.

2. Moving from status through politics to status through products

Under Mao, individuals gained status by adhering to socialist doctrine. Displaying Mao's image at home and carrying around his Little Red Book were signs of correct thinking. Those symbols are largely irrelevant to today's young urban Chinese except as kitschy fashion statements; other icons are gaining power in their place. As young Chinese come to view what they buy as symbols of their growing prosperity and engagement in modern lifestyles, products, brands and celebrities have become the newest signs of correct thinking.

China calls this generation of status-seekers the "xin xin renlei," meaning the "new" new generation. The label describes those young adults whose lifestyles include designer clothing, the latest technology, cars, pampering through spas and a host of other luxury goods and experiences. No longer limited to buying generic goods from state-owned department stores and markets, these status-conscious consumers can shop in some of the largest and most elaborate stores in the world, choosing from an expansive selection of domestic and foreign products. Although still a relatively small percentage of the population, these high-end consumers are very visible and influence a wide swath of followers who emulate them with "knock-offs." A foreigner strolling down one of Shanghai's downtown streets could leave with the impression that most of the city's population can afford Chanel sunglasses, Rolex watches, and Louis Vuitton handbags. In most cases, it would take an expert to tell that these aren't the real thing.

Facing page: In the Mao era, status came from displaying approved icons as evidence of "correct thinking" (top).

In the current era, status comes from keeping up with the latest trends, including sunglasses and fashion accessories (bottom).

Advertisers are happy to propel this dream with colorful images of modern life that shout from magazine pages, jump through TV screens, and tower over urban streets. Contrary to popular perception, advertising in China is not exclusively a chaos of characters, colors, and weirdly worded captions. Instead, some of the world's most sophisticated agencies are producing their best work, creating beautiful and compelling images designed to inspire young Chinese with both their content and their careful appreciation of Chinese sensibilities. A few still make mistakes. IKEA decorated its Chinese stores with a face largely judged to be Asian-American rather than Chinese. Nike's "Chamber of Fear" spot, featuring Cleveland Cavaliers' LeBron James battling and defeating a computer-generated Kung Fu master, insulted rather than inspired. Toyota's TV ad with ancient stone lions bowing to its Land Cruiser Prado was quickly withdrawn for offending Chinese cultural sensitivities and aggravating historical tensions between China and Japan. But these examples are rare now. At least in its urban centers, China is home to world-class advertising that has a powerful influence on demand.

A collection of billboards five stories tall in downtown Shanghai displays a beautiful young woman with gleaming skin, laughing children playing with the latest technology, and a blissful young man enjoying his new headphones.

3. Moving from "Made in China" to "Designed in China"

Since the market reforms of the late 1970s, China has gained a global reputation for mass production of cheap, often low-quality, consumer goods. If a company needs to raise its profit margins, consultants will quickly advise that management outsource whatever it can to China, pointing to the country's low-priced, educated labor force and its willingness to deal. China has also become notorious for fakes. In virtually any first-tier developed city, visitors and locals can easily find everything from imitative brands like "Giorgi Armondi" to intricately reverse-engineered knock-offs of pricey clothing, expensive watches, high-end golf clubs, and more.

No one expects this massive market of fakes to disappear suddenly or for China's manufacturing to be on par with that of Germany overnight, but China clearly is not content to be the world's cheapest copycat. From having none at all until 1982, China now boasts over 450 design schools, with hundreds more in the planning phases. Design is one of the most popular majors at Chinese universities, sending roughly 10,000 new employees a year out to hundreds of new design consulting firms opening

Some Chinese companies have become experts at copying global brands, creating products and labels that are nearly indistinguishable from the original.

offices in China and to thousands of Chinese firms seeking not to emulate but to innovate.

A few local brands are already going head to head with global brands. Lenovo, which bought IBM's personal computing division, is set to compete directly with Dell, Toshiba, and HP. Li Ning vies with Nike and Adidas for the hearts and minds of young Chinese athletes and their fans. Wahaha leads Coke and Pepsi in beverage sales throughout most of rural China. Haier, once a state-owned refrigerator manufacturer with a track record of defects, now tops the list of China's favorite brands.

A popular option, strongly encouraged by Chinese regulations, is for a foreign brand to partner with a Chinese company. This type of partnership can happen within almost any industry and with a global range of partners. Recent examples include China Putian Corporation, which partnered with Nortel on the production of cell phones; Finnish Stora Enso, which signed an agreement with Shandong Huatai Paper to manufacture paper; and Dongfeng Motor Corporation, which partnered with Japan's Nissan Motor Company to produce cars in China. Unsurprisingly, given China's ambitions, these partnerships can spawn independent competitors. Shanghai Automotive Industry Corporation initially partnered with GM and Volkswagen to build cars for the Chinese market. But the company recently announced that it had created a wholly owned subsidiary, the S.A.I.C. Motor Corporation Ltd., which will invest $1.25 billion in building new research and development centers, a car-assembly plant, and an engine factory for China and for export. This new company will have no foreign partners.

4. Moving from "developing" to leapfrogging

Only a decade ago, China suffered from infrastructural challenges that left a majority of its population without immediate access to telephone communication. Today 380 million people connect using mobile phones, according to the Chinese government's April 2005 update. That's 60 million users more than in the U.S. Similar growth is evident for other artifacts of an up-to-the-minute lifestyle. As of 2003, nearly all urban households in China owned

This five-story mall is devoted to presenting young, urban Chinese with the latest technology, electronics and appliances.

a washer, a refrigerator, and at least one color TV. More than half of urban households owned an air conditioner and a DVD player and nearly a quarter of urban households owned a personal computer.

Consumer technology and communication devices are not the only focus of China's jump into the future. On a larger scale, some of China's first-tier cities could easily be mistaken for George Jetson's hometown, Shanghai being the premier example. The city's future vision is available for all to view; at the Urban Planning Museum, a 3-D model of the metropolis sits in the center of a large room, surrounded by multimedia presentations that explain how the government will address environmental issues, traffic congestion, and other concerns many cities just hope won't happen to them. The skyline includes a replica of the Shanghai World Financial Center, soon to become the world's tallest building. This tower is surrounded for miles in all directions by a carpet of more modest, 50- to 60-story skyscrapers. As a complement to its futuristic structures, Shanghai is also home to the only commercial Maglev train in the world. Traveling at speeds up to 431 kph, the streamlined train easily outpaces the city's thousands of cabs, buses, and cars. To meet the commuting needs of its 15 million residents, the city plans to build eleven modern metro lines and ten light-rail lines over the next 25 years.

Meanwhile Beijing appears to be calmly and methodically preparing for the Olympics in 2008. Matter-of-factly outlined on the official website of the Olympic Games are its goals: to build all the sports facilities, innovate the city's transportation system, improve energy efficiency and protect the environment. When we innocently asked a Beijing local what would happen if the government couldn't achieve these ambitious goals in time, she replied simply, "That cannot happen."

Shanghai confidently portrays its future to visiting tourists and locals at the Urban Planning Museum.

2

The Power in
the Middle

The economic and developmental changes transforming China on a daily basis have created a demographic that is familiar to most Western countries but new to China. This new segment of society is the middle class.

The notion of middle class in China did not really emerge until the mid-1990s, and it's still a relatively amorphous concept. In fact, although "middle class" is loosely translated *zhong chan* in Mandarin, the expression is not widely familiar. According to the Chinese Academy of Social Sciences (CASS), if a Chinese citizen has a stable income sufficient to afford an apartment, a car, a child's education, and assorted more discretionary purchases like vacations, entertainment, and fashion, he or she is likely to be regarded as a member of the middle class. For our purposes, "middle class" would apply to a family with an annual income ranging between 30,000 to 75,000 yuan ($3,750 to $9,375 U.S.) or assets of 300,000 yuan.

Even with these criteria, it's difficult to pinpoint how many Chinese are middle class. Some analysts size the middle-class population as low as 35 million people (2.07 percent of the total population). Others, like CASS, claim it includes over 200 million people (19 percent) and is on track to reach 500 million in 2020. While the size of the country's middle class may be contested, no one disputes that it exists, is growing rapidly, and has a significant impact on China and the rest of the world.

It's this exploding middle class that is attracting marketers and developers from around the globe. This group of people—especially its youngest members—represents the new Chinese consumer class, whose promise of size and spending power intoxicates marketers. Thousands of annual reports in Europe, Japan, South Korea, the United States, and dozens of other countries reference this awakening population of young, ambitious purchasers. Thanks to them, "Expand to China" has become a standard bullet point in business plans.

Densely packed suburban flats attract millions of new middle-class families to the outskirts of China's major cities.

Fresh Influences and New Desires

We know its members are young, urban, and middle class, but what influences drive this generation of Chinese trendsetters? What is it they want?

To some extent, young people in China go through the same developmental phases as young people anywhere. They mature physically, emotionally, and cognitively, transitioning from complete dependence on their parents to at least some degree of independence as they progress from childhood to adult status. For most youth in the developed world, this phase of development expands their perspective and their personal relationships beyond the small circle of home and neighborhood to a broader world of markets, jobs, and personal relationships. The amount of time a society allows for these phases varies from culture to culture. Some, like the U.S., can tolerate an adolescence of almost two decades, starting around age 10 or 12 to a late-bloomer's youthful culmination at age 30 or so. Other, less wealthy countries usually require a much quicker coming of age.

China is somewhere in between. On the one hand, its new-found wealth and prosperity are granting the gift of extended adolescence to millions of urban young people. On the other, its traditional values and urgency to catch up economically with other countries are pressuring these same young men and women to study hard, get good jobs, and become successful. As a result, the motivations of China's youngest consumers reveal a mix of normal teenage impulses along with more mature considerations.

In our past ten years of travel and research in China, we've observed many patterns of influence and desire driving China's under-30 population. To list them all would be futile because in this current period of rapid change, the list would be obsolete before we could publish this book. However, four central tenets seem to be persistent influences on the youth culture:

1. Be an individual
2. Have new experiences
3. Connect with others
4. Help China succeed

Be an Individual

Ask any young Chinese what they want to be and you're likely to
hear them explain that they are not sure yet, but they want lives
that express their personalities and their individual uniqueness. This
might not be surprising coming from a New Yorker or young person
living in London, but until very recently, the idea that life should
reflect individual tastes was unthinkable in China. Life there was
dictated by the community, the family, and tradition. The desires
of an individual were irrelevant and potentially disruptive. But capitalism thrives on individualism, so Chinese society is adjusting to
accommodate it. In searching for their personal identity, China's
young adults are happy to be the country's guinea pigs.

That's not to say they do this easily. Long before the Maoist
era, China had a long history of collectivism that prioritized the
needs of the group over the individual. To value self-expression
is to confront deeply entrenched behaviors and beliefs, and it
would be naïve to suggest this doesn't cause tension and conflict.

*China's young middle class are the
world's newest—and soon to be
largest—group of consumers.*

Nevertheless, the trend is gaining steam and spreading well beyond the relatively sophisticated coastal cities. Right now, expressing personality is about the hottest thing a young Chinese can do.

Interestingly, the expression of youthful individualism is far more varied in China than what America and Europe experienced in the 1960s. China's teens and young adults are not rebelling en masse, adopting a pervasive counter-cultural style of defiance. How a given Chinese youth expresses his or her individualism depends on family background, income level, education, and future prospects. It also depends on whether they are new immigrants from the rural provinces hungry to prove themselves and start earning a living, or longtime urban residents eager to experience a more relaxed and easygoing life. At one extreme are young men and women who push China's cultural, social, and governmental boundaries to their limits, earning the label of *linglei* or "hooligan." At the opposite end of this continuum are the young executives,

Young Chinese are not a homogenous group. They vary in their personalities, behavior, and attitudes.

almost surgically attached to their mobile phone and PC, frantically chasing prospective business wherever it appears.

Although they express themselves in different ways, the members of China's newest generation share a common goal: finding the right path in life and then expressing that path in the things they wear, eat, buy, and do. Finding the right path can be an active search or a matter of waiting. For example, we met two young men from a rural town in Tibet who were embarking on a trip through all of China's provinces. When we asked them why, they said it was to see every part of China and learn what was happening. Once they were finished, *then* they would decide what to do with their lives. A young woman had a different philosophy about this same search, explaining that she would know the right path when she was on it. Until then, she would wait patiently. Yet another well-educated young man and his new wife were considering a riskier pursuit. They wanted to know how difficult it would be to live as illegal immigrants in the U.S. If they obeyed the laws and kept a low profile in a small city, could they avoid deportation and raise a family?

These and countless other searches for the right path are encouraged and supported by a host of local experts and a growing "self help" industry. Walk through a neighborhood community center and you'll find young people in one room taking salsa lessons, a couple learning to play piano in another, a coach offering badminton training on the grass, and English lessons underway everywhere else. China's giant-sized bookstores have entire floors devoted to self-improvement, whether that be through cooking better meals, learning new career skills, or wearing sexier lingerie. To be young and Chinese is to be a work-in-progress.

Have New Experiences

The increased personal freedom and liberation only recently available to young Chinese is not wasted on them. This is a remarkably open and optimistic generation. In a recent gathering of young men and women aged 18 to 30, we asked, "What do you fear?" When we ask this question of young adults in the U.S., we can fill pages with their concerns—everything from global warming and the war in Iraq to who will win this year's American Idol contest and will Jennifer Aniston ever find true love? Our Chinese interviewees had a simpler response: "Nothing." From their point of view, the future is filled with opportunity. It's just up to them to seek what they desire and explore new avenues that come their way. The only sure failure lies in not trying new experiences.

These new experiences come through restaurants, food stores, new luxury malls, and street vendor shops. They come through Skype, which lets them connect with friends and colleagues around the world for free, and Baidu, the Chinese competitor to Google. New experiences spring from meeting friends in a food court or from kissing a girlfriend in public and not worrying about who might be watching. They spring from TV sets and DVD players that bring new dramas and exciting celebrities into Chinese living rooms. New experiences emerge from environments like Beijing's Factory 798 in the Dashanzi Art District and the Xingtiandi in Shanghai, which have been renovated to support artistic expression. They emerge from public kiosks and booths filled with skin experts and beauty consultants ready to enlighten young consumers on the wonders of scientific testing and the latest botanical ingredients. In short, new experiences are around every corner and available every minute.

Beyond the streets of its exploding cities, Chinese citizens seek new experiences through travel. In 2005 they made over 26 million outbound trips, according to China's National Tourism Administration. By 2020, the World Tourism Organization predicts China will become the world's fourth-largest source of outbound tourists, with more than 100 million people traveling abroad each year. While shopping remains a popular reason for travel, experiencing leisure and fun is quickly gaining popularity. Similarly, current destinations now tend to be within China or nearby Asian countries such as Singapore or Thailand, but the appeal of more distant countries is growing.

Beijing's Dashanzi Art District is home to Factory 798, a facility that once produced electronics and now hosts artists, restaurants, and galleries.

Although the practice is still relatively unusual, an increasing percent of young Chinese work only long enough to afford to travel. They quit their jobs confident that they will find equivalent employment when they return. As one young Chinese woman who calls herself "Leylop" wrote in her blog:

Some people tell me I'm living the life they want. If that's what you want, why don't you go and get it for yourself? I'm not that special and I'm doing nothing extraordinary. I'm just pretty sure that I'm living for this moment rather than all these imaginary happinesses for the far future. I don't care if my retired life will be relaxing or not, I care more about my very nap in this lazy afternoon. I'm traveling again and all the money that I saved the last four months will be gone. When I come back, I'll probably lose all my contacts and need to find new jobs. But it's OK. I don't want to worry much about what might happen in the future. Enjoying the new trip is the most important thing for the moment.

Visitors to China's top sights are as likely to see groups of brightly capped local tourists as they are to see foreign travelers.

Connect with the World

China has a long tradition of *guanxiwang*, the concept of a personal connection between people in which each may prevail upon the other for a favor or service. In a recent trip from Beijing to Shanghai, we personally experienced how *guanxiwang* works. On arrival at the Beijing airport, we were greeted by a friendly baggage handler who quickly grabbed our bags, saying, "No worries, I take care you." At the ticket counter, we learned our seats were not confirmed and we had been bumped from the flight. Our new friend, the baggage handler, told us, "No worries, I fix." He led us to someone he described as his "friend," talked to him briefly, then smilingly told us, "New flight for you." He quickly marched us to the front of the China Eastern ticket line and got us on a flight leaving in 30 minutes. We proceeded to baggage check-in where he once again got us to the front of the line with a few words to another "friend." He did the same for security and for the line to board the shuttle. As our van departed for the plane, he grinned happily and said,

"Bye-bye, you very good ladies." The "very good" part no doubt had to do with the large tip we gave him, but we gladly parted with the cash because his *guanxiwang* connections saved our day.

During China's decades of stringent Communist control, these personal networks helped people acquire scarce basics. With the country's transition to a capitalist economy, the use of personal networks has changed and expanded. Now, rather than using networks to secure needed goods, young Chinese can use their personal connections to extend their social circle, find a new job, or learn about trends. They can "trade" their own connections to gain more prominence or reach within a chosen area. In the post-Mao era, personal networks have become an important tool for navigating the radical shifts in China's social order.

Thanks to modern technology, using and expanding their personal networks is simple and inexpensive for most urbanites, especially young trendsetters equipped with mobile phones and PCs. With nearly 400 million Chinese owning mobile phones and latest estimates suggesting that over 110 million Chinese can access the Internet at home, work, or in cafes, personal network connections are available any time and anyplace. These devices extend the reach of *guanxiwang* beyond what's possible face to face, introducing young Chinese to people in other parts of China and beyond the country's borders.

In addition to extending personal networks, these connections with people and countries outside of China provide efficient conduits for exchanging information, ideas, and opportunities that can instantly influence China's young urban crowd. Streaming video brings in Korean dramas and popular Western movies. Websites offer the latest computer games for download and support multiplayer gaming with competitors from around the world. Email connects international business partners. Blogs and newsgroups leak around censors and spread different points of view. The connected Chinese urbanite arguably has as much perspective on global cultures and current events as the Chinese government does and no one really knows what the population will do with this new resource in the coming decades.

Personal friendships among Chinese can become the basis of guanxiwang *connections that benefit them later in life.*

Help China Succeed

The starkest distinction between China's current youth population and other progressive youth movements in the past is its embrace of nationalism. Hippies and left-wing protestors in the U.S. and Europe burned flags and rallied against their governments in the 1960s as a key part of their countercultural identity, but China's newest generation is proud of its country and optimistic about its growth to world leadership in this century. As evidence of positive change, the young point to the construction cranes that crisscross the skylines in all of China's large cities, arcing upward like giant trend lines on a countrywide spreadsheet. They cite the 14 million new jobs China creates every year to help accommodate the rural poor pouring into coastal cities. They point to the willingness of famous brands like KFC and Starbucks to localize their offerings to better cater to Chinese sensibilities. And for good measure, they

The World Bank predicts that by 2015 half of the world's new building construction will be in China.

note the traditional cycle of luck that is scheduled to favor China as the underdog against more dominant forces such as the U.S. and Japan.

These sentiments are not the rote group-speak of comrades echoing whatever their leaders say. The expressions of national support and pride come from a heartfelt connection to the country and a belief in its promising future. As a young entrepreneur in Guangzhou nonchalantly explained, "In reality, Communism is dead. We just don't talk about it." As proof, he points to the dozens of satellite dishes sprouting from an apartment building. "It's illegal to own a satellite dish in China, but call the right person and one will be delivered tomorrow. As long as you are not disruptive, the government does not care. Our government wants to help us get rich."

Despite the clear evidence of past hardships suffered under the Chinese government, its citizens remain largely confident about its guidance and its ability to improve their lives. Disrupting the government or rebelling against its doctrine will interfere with China's global rise to power, they believe, which in turn will impede individuals' fortunes as well.

Aiguo, literally translated as "love country," is the Chinese phrase for "patriotism."

3

The New Faces of Young China

We've summed up young China's motivations in four simple principles—individuality, new experiences, social connection, and contribution to China's success—but we're not suggesting that the new Chinese consumer class is as homogenous or as easily influenced as the American consumer of the 1950's and 1960's. In fact, predicting the consumer habits of China's early adopters is particularly challenging right now because this generation is diverse and highly experimental.

With those caveats in mind, we introduce four composite characters—two young men, Wang Liang and Li Hua Min, and two young women, Ding Li and Chen Hong—who collectively represent the hundreds of young trendsetting Chinese we've met, observed, and interviewed in person over the past ten years. Though each is fictitious, building stories around their lives allows us to make them real and understandable in a way that numbers and statistics alone cannot. As such, they will reappear throughout the book to serve as examples and guides in the sections on style, food, living, and mobility, or as they would refer to those topics, *Yi Shi Zhu Xing*.

Ding Li, The Playgirl

Ding Li is 18 years old and lives to socialize with her friends. She rarely sees her busy parents, but they make sure she has plenty of money, which she happily spends on fashion and food. Her hair is streaked with copper highlights this month and her skin is pale and fair, just like her favorite Korean soap opera star, Song Hye Kyo. Her tiny dog, Xiao Bao ("little precious"), is always by her side, usually popping his head out from one of her many stylish purses.

Mornings are busy. Li has at least 30 friends to text or IM as soon as she wakes up. Picking out the day's outfit and doing her makeup usually takes at least an hour. She buys a *dan bing* (egg pancake) from a food vendor if she's running late, or eats breakfast at Yong He Da Wang and then catches a bus to work. The hour-long commute has become much more tolerable since she got her MP3 player. Her job at Esprit is fun. She talks to other girls about clothes and accessories all day. When work is not busy, she reads the fashion magazines on display for their customers.

Shopping and socializing are favorite pastimes.

She spends her evenings eating and partying with girlfriends. They're constantly hunting for a new nightclub or bar and cute boys to accompany them. Li always has a boyfriend, sometimes more than one at a time, which would make her parents very uneasy if they knew. She is not shy about meeting boys at nightclubs. She and her friends particularly enjoy going to popular clubs, like Bar Rouge in Bund 18, to mingle and practice their English with foreign travelers.

On the rare occasion that she doesn't make it out in the evening, Li hangs out in her room. Her small room is just enough for a loft bed and a desk underneath. She listens to music and chats with her friends on Instant Messenger. Most of them have

Dancing, drinking, and hanging out with friends are all part of a happy life.

webcams, so they will also communicate through those. They surf the Web together and share the latest celebrity news.

Weekends are for shopping. Li occasionally shops online at Joyo or bids for designer bags on Taobao, the Chinese version of eBay, but she prefers to cruise the large luxury malls with her boyfriend. She takes special note of the newest styles from Europe and South Korea. Her most recent purchase included a pair of Levi's, a new camera phone from Nokia, and a slimming lotion her best friend claims will really work. She loves using her camera phone to take pictures of the latest styles she sees while shopping. Li prefers large luxury malls, not just to see what's new, but also for the promotional events and product launches. She's particularly ecstatic when she stumbles upon a promotion related to cosmetics. Yesterday she went to a Revlon event on Hua Hai Road, one of Shanghai's famous shopping boulevards, and let their experts re-do her makeup.

Li doesn't think much about her future beyond next week. For now, life is too exciting and full for her to waste time worrying about marriage, careers, or politics. As long as her favorite singer, Rain, produces new songs, and her soaps continue to be available on DVDs, the future can wait.

Boyfriends are an important accessory.

Chatting on IM and browsing for products online are a popular way to pass the time.

Wang Liang, The Striver

Wang Liang is a fast-talking young executive with sharp eyes and a broad smile. He could be easily mistaken for a 15 year-old, but is actually 25. He is slim and dressed casually in a rugby shirt and khaki pants that look just like the dozens of shirts and pants he has in his flat. He dresses for success when needed, but fashion doesn't much interest Liang. What does interest him are fame, power, and money.

Liang works as an advertising salesman for one of Shanghai's large media companies. His office is about an hour commute from his flat, but he likes his new Volkswagen Dazhong Polo, so the drive doesn't bother him. When he's the boss, he'll get a car that reflects his status—something like the Audi TT Quattro or the new Mercedes that he saw at the Shanghai Auto Exhibition. But with a little luck, he believes, he won't need to work in business at all. His real goal is to become a world-famous actor, and his current job seems a reasonable path.

Ambitious and energetic, these young men see a rich future ahead of them.

A car represents a successful start to a promising life.

At the end of each work day, Liang hurries home to his flat. The 150 square-foot studio is tiny, but it's suitable for his current lifestyle. He feeds his cat and then spends the next few hours watching a favorite movie and practicing his acting craft by imitating the actors. Today his choice is Spider Man, but he also likes X-Men and any film starring Bruce Willis. New DVDs come out every week, and it's easy to pick one up from the corner vendor for less than 10 yuan ($1.25 U.S.). At last count, he had over 50 DVDs.

When the movie ends, Liang spends another four to five hours on his computer. The single room that serves as his living room, bedroom, and kitchen is filled with the latest technology. To Liang, technology is as important as food, clothing, or any other basic necessity. He can't imagine life without it. His computer has broadband access, which allows him to play online with other gamers from all over the world. His DVD player shows the latest Eminem music videos he's downloaded, and his MP3 player easily syncs with his computer to get new music files for free.

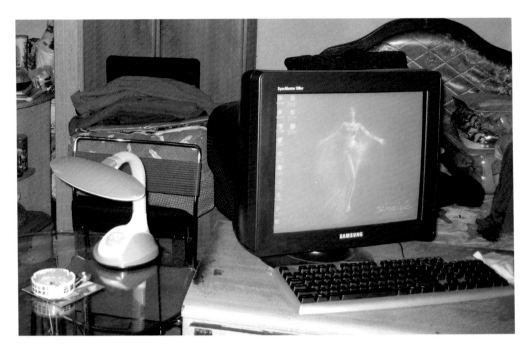

Furniture is not as important as having a new computer, DVD player, a TV, a stereo and dozens of new movies and shows.

When he's away from home, Liang's mobile phone takes the place of his computer, connecting him with a wide network of friends or playing the latest movie. A quick text message lets him know if his friends are available and where to meet them. They may go to a local karaoke bar after visiting a favorite restaurant. On the weekends, there's always a new club opening or a new DJ in town. If he stays home, he can always watch sports on TV. Although it is technically illegal, he has a satellite dish, which brings him NBA games from the U.S.

Liang loves the U.S. because it's the most powerful country in the world. He admires Bill Gates and George Bush, both of whom he sees as strong men who dominate their respective fields. One day, he will visit America. He'll see Hollywood and New York, maybe even Las Vegas. He wonders if he could just stay there, as he's heard others have done.

Sometime next year, Liang plans to marry his girlfriend and move to a larger flat that will accommodate a family. They toured a model unit at the Spring River Garden in Hongqiao last week and can buy a new three-bedroom apartment for about 750,000 Yuan (about $94,000 U.S.). His fiancée informed Liang that her parents will live with them, but the way Liang sees it, as long as he has his computer, his DVDs, a wide-screen TV, and his sports programs, life will be good.

A beautiful girlfriend or wife is a key attribute of a successful life.

Chen Hong, The Modern Conservative

Chen Hong is a reserved but articulate young woman in her last year of college. She wears her dark hair long and straight. Her elegant good looks need no makeup. She wears stylish clothing but nothing extreme. If she lived in the U.S., she'd be considered "preppy."

When she's not at school, Hong lives in a downtown flat she shares with three other girls. Her mother and father still live in her home town of Guilin, in northern Guangxi province. They have worked hard all their lives and have saved much of what they've earned, but Hong can't get them to spend on themselves. Everything they do is for her.

Hong is an average student. She didn't score high enough on the national college entrance exam to get into one of China's top universities, but she's proud of her design major and believes it sets her

Driven and dedicated, these young people see education as their ticket to success.

The future holds a rich and colorful life for those who are willing to work for it.

apart from others. She's not sure what career to pursue, but she's confident it should be in advertising, PR, or marketing because those professions offer challenges and excitement. She doesn't want a job where she's doing the same thing over and over again.

Her one-room flat barely accommodates the beds and desks she and her roommates share, but the young women don't spend much time there. Hong rises early on weekdays and rides her bike to campus, where she spends most of her day either in class or in the library. After school, she bikes to her part-time job as a translator for a Chinese company with many American clients. She's happy to have the job, as employment is getting more difficult for young, educated Chinese like her. Still, it's demanding; this week she's worked every night until at least 11P.M.

The weekends are easier. On Saturdays, Hong usually window shops with her friends or hangs out at a teahouse or cafe. On Sundays, she always has dinner with her aunt and uncle who live in the suburbs. She has a boyfriend, but their relationship is not serious yet. Although premarital sex is allowed, the government forbids marriage for undergrads. Like her parents, she respects the advice of the government and other authorities, and she never wants to behave badly in the eyes of society. She is ashamed of the young people she sees who are loud and disruptive in public or who dress suggestively, because in her view they reflect poorly on China. Nevertheless, she cherishes her personal freedom and can't imagine what life was like under Mao.

Hong loves and admires her parents, but she doesn't want the life they have led. They have worked too hard and sacrificed too much. She would like to marry someday, but she does not want children. Children are a great burden in China. She can not have the rich and colorful life she dreams of having and still support a family. She and her husband will be happy working a moderate amount and spending their free time traveling around the world.

Friends are important for support and companionship.

Li Hua Min, the Rule Breaker

At 20, Li Hua Min is glad to be out of school. He wasn't interested in attending college, even if he had been accepted. His parents still support him and provide him enough spending money to hang out with his friends at the nightclubs, bars, and shopping malls in Guangzhou. Like his idol, Eminem, Hua Min has a tattoo. He has bleached and dyed his hair a bright shade of orange, and last week had his lip pierced. His parents aren't happy about his personal style or the way he spends his time, but what can they do? He's a proud member of China's *linglei* crowd—a "hooligan."

Hua Min's mobile phone directory is filled with names of friends and acquaintances he's met while tending bar in one of the city's many bars and clubs. His job and the after-hour parties last well into the night, so Hua Min rarely wakes before noon. Self-expression through appearance is extremely important to him, so he takes his time getting ready in the morning—sculpting his hair with various products, choosing the right outfit and picking the right pair of sunglasses from the collection on his dresser.

Hua Min is on the street by 2P.M., smoking a cigarette while he text-messages friends to learn where everyone will be tonight. Later in the afternoon, he may stop by and see a friend who's a hair stylist or another who runs an Internet café, to compare notes on the best DJs, newest drinks, or latest club openings.

As evening approaches, Hua Min usually takes a nap to recharge for the night. On his nights off, he and his friends can easily make

Every day is a new adventure with no goals and few boundaries.

stops at three or four different clubs. They seek out local places and avoid anything too mainstream, where the foreigners and business executives go. Sometimes they start the night playing games at an arcade. Before making their rounds at bars and clubs, they will fill up on food. Their eating preferences are simple. They will make a quick stop for a bowl of noodles or sample street food at the night market. Lately, they have been checking out some local electronic clubs. Hua Min has made a few friends there who have been supplying him with the drug Ecstasy. He and his friends know they run a risk of getting caught, but they enjoy the temporary escape.

Friends represent connections to parties, bars, internet cafes, DJs, and other exciting new experiences.

For Hua Min, life moves fast. Friends come and go. Bars and clubs change. Styles rise and fall. The best way to show that he's keeping up with all of this is to have the latest mobile phone. Fortunately, it's easy to sell his old one on Taobao, China's local version of eBay, so he's happy to upgrade often. Right now, life is about fun and experimentation. Life would not be meaningful if it revolved around only work and making and saving money, the way his parents' lives do. As long as he's connected to the ever-expanding network of young, cool Chinese, the future won't leave him behind.

The Internet connects to a world that's even bigger and faster-moving than the streets of China.

4

Yi

Shi

Zhu

Xing

衣食住行

T

The ancient Chinese saying, "Yi Shi Zhu Xing" is literally translated as "clothing, food, housing, and transport," but people use it to express the essential requirements of life. For most of the 20th century, China's masses struggled to acquire these basic needs, but today, as China's economy charges relentlessly forward and begins to deliver on promised riches, upwardly mobile young Chinese like those we met in the previous chapter no longer worry about basic staples. For them, these four areas represent opportunities to express their new individualism and to display evidence of their improving circumstances. Clothing is no longer just about modesty, durability, and protection from the elements. It's now a means of portraying personality through brand choice and style. Food is no longer just about nutrition and familial well-being. It's also a way to experience cosmopolitanism through foreign restaurants and imported food. Housing means more than mere shelter, as it now supports private, personal lives separate from extended families and free of state oversight. Mobility is not just about getting from one place to another. It's become a symbol of freedom.

As these fundamental necessities have evolved into expressions of lifestyle, their purchase has similarly progressed from an obligatory chore to a multi-phased selection process. When only one style of white refrigerator existed, the only decision was

A designer merges traditional Chinese fashion with modern pop culture symbolism to create a dress that expresses an aesthetic combining old values and new images.

A restaurant invites customers to experience "post-industrial" Western-style dining.

Motorcycles and other forms of transport must attract with design, color and brand, not just function and price.

Personal style extends beyond individuals to homes and furnishings.

whether or not to own one. Shopping was not an issue; buying a refrigerator involved saving enough money, making the purchase, and installing it. With dozens of available styles and an abundance of colors and features, choosing the right refrigerator involves many more steps and much greater consideration. Function and price are still important, but so are quality, design, size, and shape. Brand becomes important, both for what it says about the product and what it implies about the purchaser. As these new attributes gain importance, and as more companies bring greater choice to the market, China's young consumers face something their parents rarely, if ever, did: choosing which products and experiences best fit their personality and lifestyle. Are they the type of person who would buy a blue refrigerator with a wine door? Does a bright orange motorcycle or white leather boots with 3-inch heels reflect their character?

Book titles reflect the burgeoning choices in China for different art, design, music, and fashion experiences.

Advertisers are only too happy to help these new consumers make decisions by introducing them to brand imagery. Lifestyle ads three stories tall wallpaper buildings all over China's main cities, decorating them with the placid smiles of beautiful Asian and Western women representing companies like Estée Lauder, L'Oreal, Shiseido, and Avon. Posters touting a club's new DJ lineup or latest theme night are plastered with logos from sponsors like Nokia, Chivas, and Carlsberg. In the heart of shopping malls, shapely models wearing branded uniforms demonstrate the latest weight-reduction devices or hand out coupons for the newest store. Popular television celebrities act as spokespersons for all kinds of goods and services, instructing young viewers about which brand of skin-whitening cream to buy, which new restaurant to patronize, and which mobile phone will make them most attractive and fashionable.

The imagery and tactics are intended to help Chinese consumers associate brands with lifestyles, and they can be effective when well executed. If a young consumer is trendy, playful, and carefree like our character Ding Li, right now she will be attracted to brands connected with the Korean Wave influence or luxury brands like Louis Vuitton and Chanel. To a consumer who, like Chen Hong, favors a more conservative style, or like Wang Liang, is more ambitious, brands representing success and achievement will seem appealing. Consumers with a rebellious streak, like our Li Hua Min, will seek brands that represent a more nonconformist stance, such as those favored by an underground rock band or celebrities like the scandal-prone Nicholas Tse or edgy Faye Wong. Each will choose the brands or experiences that best fit his or her current lifestyle, using advertisements as a guide.

If you're thinking this sounds a little too pat and predictable, let us now introduce the wildcard. Brand marketing is proving effective in China, but the young consumers are quickly learning to rely on a form of endorsement that is hard to control but can result in skyrocketing popularity— a friend's recommendation that something is "cool."

Discussions of who or what is cool fuel millions of text messages, blog postings, and table chat in China. "Cool" in Chinese is a borrowed word. It's translated as *ku* in Mandarin, a phonetic version of the English word. *Ku* is a young word in China, with too brief a history to have developed deep cultural roots or shades of nuance. As such, it is not as pervasive a term as it is in the U.S. or other Western countries. The concept of coolness is appreciated by young Chinese and increasingly relevant as their lives become less about basic economic struggle and more about defining meaning and identity in a rapidly changing society. They just don't have a strict definition or set attitude about who or what is cool. Currently, it tends to be applied to products, services, experiences, and people who adopt a non-conformist style. That behavior alone is cool.

At present, virtually any nonconformist stance is considered "cool."

If deciding who or what is cool seems like idle gossip and chitchat, consider the uniqueness of the Chinese consumer market: hundreds of millions of consumers growing wealthier, and hence more able to consume, all connected through an intricate system of social networks facilitated by cell phones and the Internet. If Ding Li or someone like her decides it's cool to buy Wahaha cola instead of Coke, she can instantly influence her entire network, which through its interconnections may stretch to thousands of other young girls and boys like her. If that scenario isn't enough to wreck the sleep of corporate executives, imagine what will happen as these networked consumers with well-honed bargaining skills become aware of their group purchasing power.

In the chapters that follow, we explore the emerging sensibilities and future desires of these young consumers in the four areas that offer them the greatest ability to express themselves: style, food, living and mobility. In each chapter, we briefly examine the historical context or any other influencing forces and then discuss the transformations that strike us as most important, whether driven by companies, consumers or the Chinese government. Sit back and enjoy the journey. Ding Li, Chen Hong, Wang Liang, and Li Hua Min are happy to accompany us and share their experiences along the way.

5

yi (style)

衣

The literal translation of Yi is "clothing," but to capture the changes reshaping Chinese culture, we have expanded the definition to cover a wider perspective on style. Clothing is an important focus of China's young trendsetters, but so are accessories, cosmetics and shopping environments.

Chinese teens and young adults pay far greater attention to fashion and to their personal image than their parents' generation ever did or ever could. Some experts credit this explosion of interest and enthusiasm to pent-up demand created by decades of restraint under Communist rule. Others with equal expertise on the country believe it's a natural expression of freedom and experimentation by young people who are better educated, wealthier, and better connected with worlds beyond their borders than any previous generation in China.

Both conditions likely contribute to the pervasive quest for style, but for young Chinese, money spent on fashion—whether clothing, beauty products, or cosmetic surgery—is not just an expression of vanity or whim; instead, it's an investment in the future. Today's "20-something" Chinese will explain that a more striking appearance can result in a better job or a higher salary. A prettier face can attract more and better marriage prospects. To them, spending money in pursuit of these goals is not only justified, it's admirable.

Changing Perceptions of Beauty

Every culture has its ideal of personal beauty that reflects its values and norms. As a culture's values change, its perception of who and what are beautiful changes as well. For some cultures, this change is a slow, steady evolution; for others, the shift is rapid and dramatic. China is experiencing a little bit of both.

Some longstanding standards of beauty continue to exert significant influence today. For example, the appeal of fair skin is driving tremendous growth of skin-whitening products. This is not, as some might assume, a desire to imitate Caucasian or Western norms; the pursuit of fair skin is actually an ancient Chinese tradition. What's surprising is that contemporary Chinese women continue to believe that lighter skin is a symbol of feminine beauty and can compensate for other perceived flaws, such as a large nose or wide face.

Ding Li loves to watch her favorite new Korean soap opera "Full House." The drama has captured the attention of all her friends and she looks forward to getting the DVD copies as soon as they reach her neighborhood. If only she could look like Song Hye Kyo, the lead actress. She's cut and styled her hair to look like Song's, and she's found similar clothing at the local mall. But the actress's perfectly shaped face, double eyelids, and high cheekbones would insure her future success, both at work and in love. Plastic surgery is the answer. Her boyfriend has hinted about a special Valentine's gift for her. Hopefully, this is what he has in mind.

Some standards of beauty are constant. Chinese have long idealized pale skin, and soaring sales of skin whiteners indicate this preference remains popular.

一白遮三醜

*"Fairness hides
three flaws"*

Other modern beauty practices are departures from the past. The Cultural Revolution from 1966 to 1976 dismissed personal beauty as irrelevant. In its place, women were expected to embrace "revolutionary beauty" as illustrated by the ever-present gray Mao suit and short, unisex hairstyles. Both sexes' individuality was inhibited, but women in particular had little ability to express themselves through style or cosmetics. Although the revolution's dictates were not as severe as China's earlier practice of foot binding, they nonetheless constrained women to a prescribed standard of beauty.

The opening of China in the 1980s fostered new ideals of beauty initially influenced by American, European, and Japanese entertainment media. As China's economy improved and as young people began to have contact with their peers around the world, style influences broadened and had even more impact. In a pendulum swing that tests the laws of physics, the population of China went from wearing a generic and singular revolutionary look to trying just about every new fashion fad on the planet. A growing percentage of young women and men are expressing their individuality in everything from their hair color to their mobile phone covers.

The young girls wearing short skirts and boots are similar to their U.S. counterparts. The angled cut and brightly dyed locks of some young college students—men and women—are identical to looks popular in Korea. The tiny pet dog and Gucci bag on the arm of a young Chinese woman could just as easily belong to a young Japanese woman, and the well-cut conservative suit you see on an ambitious young Chinese executive is no different from those worn by his European colleagues.

What's distinctive about style in China, however, is that it incorporates *all* of these looks and integrates them in a way that is quintessentially Chinese. This comes as no surprise to those familiar with China's history. For thousands of years, the country has excelled at integrating the features of other cultures into the traditional Chinese way of life and using those outside influences to refine or revive its core culture. This current fascination and experimentation with global fashion has deep-seated roots which may explain why it doesn't seem threatening to older Chinese.

During the Cultural Revolution, personal style and beauty were not highly regarded. There was one prescribed look and little tolerance for individuality. Some older citizens retain the old look.

Fashionable Chinese girls shopping at a mall in Shanghai could easily be mistaken for trendy young Americans.

This young girl has bobbed and dyed her hair to emulate the street fashions popular in Seoul.

Some young Chinese women pamper their dogs as much as themselves.

A young Chinese executive dons global "dress for success" attire.

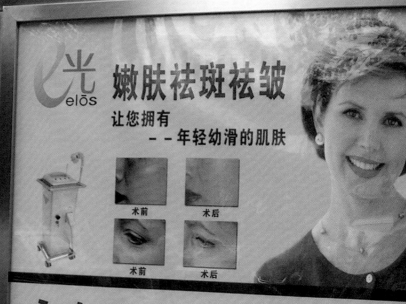

Not everyone is participating in this change to the same extent. Across China this stylistic evolution is occurring to varying degrees and at various rates of change. The most obvious leaders are white-collar "office ladies" who are in their 20's and have disposable income. Teenage girls from middle or upper class families are equally fashion savvy, although they must wear uniforms to school. Some young men have entered the fray as China's version of "metrosexuals," appropriately called *ai-mei nanren* or "love-beauty men." Shanghai and Guangzhou, benefiting from their proximity to trendy Hong Kong, are far more fashion-forward than Beijing, and all of the large coastal cities are ahead of their rural inland counterparts. But despite its unequal distribution, the trend towards greater emphasis on fashion seems to be spreading broadly as evidenced by the growing number of local and national beauty pageants recently introduced after 54 years of prohibition, including "Miss Artificial Beauty," all of whose contestants have had cosmetic surgery.

In addition to the influence of North American, European, and Japanese media, other influences are persuading millions of young Chinese that traditional standards of beauty can be updated and enhanced with a mix of modern looks. One of the hottest current influences on fashion and perceptions of beauty is South Korea. Even though many of these creatively designed and brightly colored fashions are actually manufactured in China, the prestige of Korean styling makes an item instantly desirable. Termed the "Korean Wave," or *Hanliu* in Mandarin, this influence can be seen throughout the full range of Chinese pop culture.

Some experts suggest that Korean style can be thought of as Western style "lite," meaning it's a dilution or filtering of Western values that are too extreme for China right now. We see the culture's current fascination with Korean style as a desire for novelty tied to familiar Eastern values. As with all style trends, we expect it to evolve beyond emulation as Chinese youth become more experienced and confident in expressing their individualism.

Facing page: This ad encourages Chinese women to use surgery to improve their appearance.

Chinese consumers are experimenting with looks from many countries, although currently Korean style is arguably the most popular. The sign above this busy shopping area reads "Korean Market."

Another influence on China's changing perceptions of beauty that shouldn't be underestimated is the growing presence and power of cosmetics advertising. The beauty industry in China is enormous—over 170 billion yuan, or approximately $21 billion U.S., according to a 2004 report by leading Chinese economists—with a five-year average growth rate in excess of 20 percent per year. Media reports rank it as the fifth-largest industry in the country, topped only by property, cars, tourism, and technology. Over 4000 personal care product companies currently vie for consumer attention in China, including global players like Procter & Gamble, L'Oreal, and Unilever. Media spending drives growth in this market, so ads proliferate in magazines, on billboards and in almost any other space that will support them.

Fashion ads proliferate in magazines, on billboards, and in almost any other space that will support them.

Many of these ads feature Western or Westernized faces with large eyes and lighter hair. Critics sometimes characterize this as an effort to force conformity to an international ideal, but we see a simpler motive. At this time in China's development the Western world represents prosperity. By featuring Westernized faces in their ads, cosmetic companies associate their product with that prosperity and higher status. The women (and some men) who buy these products are not trying to look Western, merely aspiring to the successful lifestyle these icons represent.

It's too early to identify a new Chinese style of beauty or even a tendency toward a particular look. At this point, what we see is experimentation along many different paths and a delicate balancing act between what is possible and what is allowed or accepted. China is trying to create its own aesthetic around beauty and style, rather than copying or adapting those of other nations. When a truly Chinese style finally emerges, it will most likely be a hybrid of various Asian and Western influences, and it could in turn influence the rest of the world.

Many beauty ads feature Western or Westernerized faces in an attempt to associate the advertised product with prosperity and higher status.

The Newest Beauty Ingredient: Science

Chinese women have traditionally looked to herbs and other natural ingredients for their cosmetic and personal-care needs. They continue to do that, but with the rise of modernity and the growing influence of celebrity endorsements and global brands, science plays an increasingly important role. Whether it's plastic surgery, makeup, or specialized ingredients, young Chinese women increasingly favor those approaches that provide documented proof of their effectiveness.

The most obvious appeal of science is its association with a contemporary Western or global lifestyle. Science implies a rigorous process with specific proof points, not a folkloric mystery passed from mother to daughter. Although many popular products continue to contain natural ingredients, their packaging, advertising and direct selling points emphasize the testing process or other means of improved efficacy. As young Chinese consumers search for the best skin whitener or acne cure, the science angle is new and offers a distinct choice compared to the more traditional products offered in the herbal shops. Products and services that emphasize a scientific connection and provide this type of information tend to come from Europe, Japan, and the U.S., further reinforcing the idea that science and success go hand in hand.

Ding Li searches through Rayli, her favorite beauty magazine, looking for a new lotion that will whiten her skin. The array of products on the pages is overwhelming. Normally she seeks her mother's advice, but in this case, her mother will be no help. She will just recommend a trip to the neighborhood herbal pharmacy to buy the same concoctions she uses. Those old ginseng creams aren't as effective or as safe as the new formulas. They don't have the scientific testing or the latest ingredients. Maybe Gloria Lin, the beauty consultant at the L'Oreal counter can help her find the right products.

Herbs and other natural ingredients have been a key feature in Chinese cosmetic and personal-care products for centuries.

New beauty products include natural ingredients but emphasize scientific efficacy and lifestyle positioning.

Science also implies speed or efficiency—modern ways are faster. A consumer can trade money for time, and for a young Chinese woman eager to catch up with the rest of the world, this is a fair trade. The boom in cosmetic surgery is an example of this desire for immediate change. For about 20,000 yuan (approximately $2,500 U.S.), a young college graduate can undergo surgery to make her face more oval—a choice she feels will help her land a better job. A teenager may opt for the popular double-fold eyelid operation to please her boyfriend or to copy her girlfriends. The procedures have become so commonplace among wealthy and middle-class young people that surgery centers prepare in advance for the annual peak that occurs during students' summer vacation.

With so many choices of novel ingredients and new procedures, young Chinese are quickly overwhelmed with the product and service selection and actively seek education or advice. Few can turn to a mother or aunt for this because older women in China have little familiarity with these methods. Companies have been quick to fill the information void, providing sales consultants,

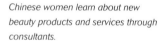

Chinese women learn about new beauty products and services through consultants.

image advisors, celebrity endorsements, and brand positioning that highlights the scientific underpinnings of a product or service.

Consultants can become trusted advisors who regularly instruct and influence their clients' choices. They may influence through word of mouth or use company-provided documentation. Packaging and pamphlets can play a similar role if they explain how ingredients work or if they reference a scientifically based research-and-development process for creating new products.

Being Seen: The Role of the Mega Mall

Shopping has always been a public experience in China. Traditionally, it involved colorful, open-air markets with fresh meat, produce, and wares for customers who had to bargain hard. The decades under Mao's Communism saw dreary stores providing few choices, and clerks with no incentive to sell. But all that has changed in recent years. According to retail analysts, in the last six years more than 400 large malls have been built in China. Within two or three years, China will be home to seven of the ten largest shopping malls in the world.

These new malls offer more comprehensive shopping environments that usually include entertainment complexes and restaurants as well. They offer customers more selection, more opportunity for comparison shopping, easy exposure to what's new both from window shopping and people watching, and more opportunity to be seen. As such, the shopping mall is quickly becoming a new social arena in which a young Chinese girl or boy can experiment with identity. For millions of young Chinese, these malls represent the perfect meeting spot. They are not politically controlled, so youngsters feel freer to experiment with new looks or behaviors that might push acceptable limits. In a sense, the malls offer the first true public life in China in many years.

Chen Hong walks to the Golden Resources mall near her home in Beijing. The five-story building is not as elaborate as the new South China mall in Dongguan, but nevertheless it is her favorite public place. She can rarely afford anything sold in the thousand or more stores it contains, but to her the mall is like a giant magazine, filled with the latest trends in popular culture. She and her friends buy ice cream and walk past the clustered stores seeing the fashions from Korea, the cosmetics from France, the movies from America. When she sees something she wants, it's usually easy to find it much cheaper from a local vendor where she can use her bargaining skills to get an even lower price.

Cavernous malls filled with brands from around the world are popping up in all of China's major urban centers.

Young Chinese socialize outside the store of the Xidan shopping district.

Unfortunately for their investors, mall traffic does not necessarily result in high sales. Young Chinese treat these retail megalopolises like fashion magazines—a place to learn about new styles and trends, but not necessarily a place to buy. In most cases, the items offered in the mall are too pricey for the majority of local customers enjoying the climate-controlled environment, and bargaining is not allowed at the large, established brand stores. Close copies of even the most recently introduced fashions are readily available at a fraction of the price from street vendors or vendors stationed in less upscale malls. These retailers are happy to haggle over the right price if it will result in a sale. If they are lucky, a less knowledgeable Western tourist will pay close to full price.

Knock-offs are readily available from street vendors at a fraction of the original's price.

According to government data, retail sales in China have jumped nearly 50 percent in the last four years, but while Chinese have more money to spend, it's not clear yet if the generation now in its trend-conscious twenties will become the world's newest consumers or revert to the traditional Chinese habit of saving. In 2005, Credit Suisse First Boston forecast that spending by Chinese consumers would quintuple in the next ten years to $3.7 trillion, but that same year a *McKinsey Quarterly* report showed saving rates rising rather than declining. We doubt if anyone has an accurate crystal ball for this behavior. The Chinese ability to spend relatively freely is simply too new for anyone to predict its long-term projection.

Whether or not young Chinese men and women embrace consumerism as their Western, Korean, and Japanese counterparts have, their penchant for style is likely to follow them into adulthood. It may settle down into a more moderate mode, or it may continue to be a vehicle for experimentation and self expression. Either way, if style retains its reputation as a good investment, the Mao jacket and unisex haircut are unlikely to return.

A young Chinese girl experiments with a new look.

6

Shi (food)

食

Food, or *shi*, has been a central focus of Chinese life for thousands of years. "Have you eaten yet?" is a common greeting, and "You've gotten fatter!" is a welcome compliment. These salutations reflect centuries of concern about getting enough food and the related value the Chinese place on eating well. The country's most recent famines occurred during Mao's rule, and the majority of Chinese lived on a basic and meager diet during this period. In cities, food was still rationed as late as the 1980s due the country's stagnant agricultural sector and closed borders.

After Mao's death in 1976, the Chinese government initiated agricultural reforms to revive its food production. These actions, along with admission to the World Trade Organization in 2001 and continuing efforts to lower trade barriers, helped China go from rations to abundance in less than 30 years. As a result, most of China's children, teens, and young adults living in major cities today have experienced no shortages only a wealth of food delivered through modern retailers, convenience channels, and a flood of new restaurants. The country's growing affluence, its exposure to outside influences, and its desire for experimentation has created an appetite for new flavors, new ingredients, and new eating experiences—all of which marketers and restaurateurs from around the world are happy to feed.

New Food: The World on a Plate

Chinese cuisine represents one of the finest and most varied culinary traditions in the world. It benefits from thousands of years of development and the contributions of many different geographic regions and cultural influences. Each province has developed its own unique cuisine, typically reflecting agricultural, geographic, cultural, and foreign influences too numerous and detailed to summarize. At the simplest level, a Chinese meal consists of a starch accompanied by numerous meat, fish, and vegetable dishes. In the northern provinces, the starch is more likely to be noodles or buns, while southern provinces will serve rice. Variations on thousands of details of preparation, cooking, and presentation add elaborate dimension to this basic foundation. To the average Chinese citizen, regardless of income level or educational background, food is an essential pleasure in life. To them, the adage "Food is heaven" is not hyperbole.

Multiple plates of fresh, flavorful vegetables, meats, and fruits accompany the staple foods of rice, noodles, or buns.

It's Sunday night, and 23 year-old Wang Liang knows his parents are crowded around a large table with other family members. Soon his mother will carry a steaming plate of freshly made pork dumpling to the gathered clan who will already be feasting on dishes of cold cuts, strawberries, almonds, green vegetables, and rice. The meal will be carefully balanced to include the right combination of "hot," "cold," "wet," and "dry" elements to restore bodily harmony. Everyone will happily share the dishes while discussing their children's lives. This comforting familial scene has been repeated weekly all his life, but Liang isn't joining them tonight. His new job keeps him working on an erratic schedule so nowadays he rarely has time for a traditional meal. Luckily his refrigerator is stocked with packaged meals he found at the new Carrefour. Convenience stores are popping up all along his commute route. His office just installed a series of vending machines, and a banquet of warm or cold food lies waiting outside on vendors' pushcarts. If he works too late, he can stop into a restaurant that stays open 24 hours a day. If he's with friends, they can experience one of the new theme restaurants that open weekly. While Liang loved having all his meals prepared by his parents, the new food scene in China is almost as good, and comes with less guilt and obligation.

"Food is Heaven"

The preparation and consumption of food in China does more than fill bellies. Chinese have long believed food to have curative powers beyond its nutrient or caloric value. Ingredients and dishes are tied to regional and social group identity to ethical beliefs. Eating rituals communicate feelings and familial connections beyond what words and characters can convey. Even perceptions of power and status mix seamlessly with the elements of daily meals.

For young urban Chinese who grew up taking their meals at a communal table, food and eating remain highly symbolic. Meals continue to be a time for socializing and a means of expressing status. Even trendy diners worry about combining the right food properties, and Chinese from the southern provinces would never order seven dishes because that is what they serve the "spirited aways" when honoring their departed ancestors. But despite food's already extensive role, it is expanding even further for this generation. For them, food directly reflects the changing world around them with all its new diversity and its profusion of choice.

Books explain how the right food can improve health.

Young Chinese walking down any main thoroughfare in Guangzhou, Beijing, Wuhan, Shanghai, or other major cities encounter new food options at almost every step. Street vendors hawk traditional favorites like candied fruit, oranges, and baked yams, or they sell newly popular carbonated sodas, yogurt, and bottled water. For the more affluent, tea shops like R.B.T. have become as commonplace as Starbucks. Local grocers tempt shoppers with sidewalk displays of imported fruit, and global superstores build towers of brightly packaged products from every continent. Although most twenty-something consumers say they prefer the traditional Chinese cuisine they ate as children, they are more than willing take a food "adventure" and try a dish from Brazil, India, Thailand, Korea, and dozens of other countries.

This eager exploration of new tastes has turned China's food industry into a trend-driven business. New food and beverage concepts explode in popularity for a period of time and then quickly die as the next new food, flavor, or restaurant appears on the scene. Locals joke that the worst business in China is to run a restaurant. The business can die overnight because customers have become so fickle and no one can predict what they will want next.

Influences driving these rapid-fire trends come from many sources. As workers migrate from China's rural provinces to take jobs in the growing urban centers, they seek out their native regional foods. These tastes spill over to the population at large and begin reshaping a locale's cuisine. Spicy meals normally associated with the Hunan province or the preserved ingredients more common in northeastern China mingle with Cantonese dishes that originated in the south. Foreign restaurants add their influence by introducing foods that are completely new to China, like tacos and French fries. They may take a popular dish and prepare it in a new way, as KFC did with its "spring chicken rolls," or they may introduce a new theme or eating environment, such as McDonald's and TGI Friday's have done.

Similarly, retailers' displays of goods in their aisles and on endcaps are continual and pervasive sources of influence, helped along by merchandising tags that proclaim "new taste," "new

New restaurants line streets and malls attracting customers with their trendy environments and modern messages.

Busy street vendors serve whatever new food the crowd is buying.

Western-style restaurants have proliferated in coastal cities and now are spreading to smaller cities in the West and North.

New foods from around the world crowd grocery shelves, tempting shoppers looking for the latest taste experiences.

flavor," or "imported." Print and broadcast advertising stir demand to a froth by associating the consumption of new foods with living a successful, affluent life. Global brands like Coca-Cola and Nestlé are happy to respond to the latest craze since the early-adopter population is nearly the size of the entire U.S.

In addition to importing new varieties of food, these marketers have also introduced the concept of branded convenience food to China's young shoppers, encouraging them to buy prepared noodles, pre-cooked meats, and instant beverages from a company that recognizes and supports their new lifestyles. In doing this, they've brought forth the idea that food is more than its content; its form, packaging, and symbolism are all important. In this role, food marketers now join the family and the school in contributing to a Chinese child's education in the practical, social, and symbolic values of food.

The ability of China's food market to generate and accommodate these influences represents another miracle of reform. Until very recently, China's burgeoning food industry was dominated by thousands of small shops and open-air "wet markets" selling fresh produce, fish, and live poultry. The country's warehousing and

The term "imported" is considered synonymous with "new" and "modern."

Global brands like Coca-Cola have introduced the idea that a food's form,
packaging and symbolism are as important as its ingredients.

distribution system was fragmented, outdated, and in many cases, controlled by the government. This effectively discouraged retailers from Europe and the U.S. from entering the country, even after other regulatory hurdles were resolved. But all that has changed. From just one supermarket in 1990, according to a 2003 report by the Chinese Chain Store and Franchise Association, the country now boasts over 60,000 stores, with an estimated $71 billion in sales. Modern merchants like Wal-Mart and Carrefour now represent approximately 30 percent of the urban food market and are growing at astronomical rates.

On the restaurant side, at last count China had over 20,000 Western-style food establishments on the mainland with thousands more opening every year. The label "Western" may be misleading, since these restaurants represent a vast range of foreign cuisines including Italian, Mexican, American, French, Arabic, Russian, Swiss, Turkish, Canadian, Dutch, Brazilian, and German. While most common in the affluent coastal cities and other major urban areas, these restaurants are rapidly spreading throughout China in response to seemingly unlimited demand.

In rural China, wet markets are still a common means of buying produce, fish, and poultry. In urban areas, however, they are being replaced by giant supermarkets.

During Mao's regime, most grocery stores were state-owned and had little incentive to improve their offerings. Today grocery stores compete aggressively to attract customers.

Ding Li enters the new Pizza Hut off Hua Hai Road. Inside it's crowded with young Chinese, including about a dozen of her friends. They are all fashionably dressed. Some talk on mobile phones, others chat and laugh in small groups, and one couple sits quietly holding hands in full public view. As always, the center of attention is not the pizza, but the salad bar. Li and her friends surround the display of traditional Western salad ingredients and excitedly begin building salad "towers" from the array of vegetables and fruit. One friend balances a slice of watermelon on two sticks of celery and tops it with a scaffolding of carrots and a lettuce roof. Another follows a specific color scheme. Li snaps photos as each masterpiece is carefully returned to the table and the friends lightheartedly assess structure, detail, and creativity. Like so many new experiences Li encounters, this salad bar is yet another way to express individual personality.

New Restaurants: A Place for Individualism

Ask young urban Chinese to describe a traditional restaurant and they will typically list several positive attributes. They'll note that these restaurants have catered to the Chinese preference for ordering many dishes and sharing with one another, rather than eating individual portions on their own. As a result, these establishments often embody positive connotations of family and connectedness. In addition, young Chinese proudly affirm that traditional Chinese restaurants have long been known for the high quality of the food they offer and the large quantities.

Ask where traditional Chinese restaurants fail to measure up, and these same young people will also respond quickly and convincingly suggest these businesses are not known for their customer service and that they often fall short of the cleanliness standards set by the new Western-style restaurants. Further, many

Traditional Chinese restaurants have long catered to communal eating habits and as such they represent positive connotations of family and connectedness.

have unattractive interiors that pale in comparison to the trendy themed eating spots that populate each new development and mall.

For young urban Chinese, restaurants are no longer simply a place to share food with family. Like China's massive fashion malls, restaurants have become popular places to hang out with friends and socialize—places to see and be seen. Since most of these young people still live at home or share tiny flats that are too small to entertain a group of people, restaurants have become their extended dining room and their living room. As such, restaurants need to offer much more than food to capture the attention of young urban Chinese.

The proprietors of new-wave foreign restaurants springing up in major urban cities (and Chinese restaurants emulating them) are happy to serve up an environment where young diners can experiment with modern behaviors and identities. These restaurants, particularly Western-style fast-food establishments like KFC, Pizza Hut, McDonald's, and Starbucks, provide the perfect staging area for socializing and expressing romantic relationships, professional status, and contemporary child-rearing approaches. To a "cool" young Chinese man or woman, eating at the right restaurant

New-style restaurants offer stimulating environments that support the desire of young Chinese to socialize.

can be as much a fashion statement as wearing the latest outfit or using the hippest mobile phone.

If we asked our young Chinese trendsetter to describe the appeal of new style restaurants in China, he or she would explain that these establishments serve more sophisticated food in terms of composition and presentation. He'd note that the overall décor and customer service have changed to create a more holistic dining experience. He'd suggest that the innovation is more in the presentation, the service, and the environment, than in the ingredients themselves. He'd also tell you this pursuit of innovation has unleashed a competitive zeal worthy of the Iron Chef contenders. As a result, new restaurants try to outdo others with their creativity or concept, delivering a seemingly unending flow of novel restaurants and inventive cuisines.

Western-style restaurants provide young Chinese a haven where they can lounge, flirt, socialize, and try out their new identities, away from the observant eyes of their parents.

As customer service becomes more important, businesses are devoting more efforts in training their staff. This group of over 50 people cheered in unison after listening to a two minute inspirational speech from the manager about customer service.

Searching for a unique niche that will attract an affluent urban crowd, the Green T. House in Beijing serves exquisitely designed entrees, all of which use some form of tea as an ingredient. On a similar quest for distinction, the South Beauty chain offers a four-part dessert, each representing part of a Chinese calligraphy set: the brush, the ink, paper, and stone. A popular restaurant in Shanghai distinguishes itself through experience. Its entrance has no obvious door or sign. Customers learn of it through word of mouth, make a reservation by phone, and get a password that changes everyday. When they arrive at the address, they must enter that day's code by putting their hand in holes in the right sequence to gain entrance. To perform this action requires that all patrons be sober and not dyslexic, but apparently this hasn't detracted from the restaurant's appeal.

New restaurants often must go to extremes to attract the fickle crowd of affluent customers. A beautiful but highly unusual grass couch complements the uniquely designed entrees at Green T. House in Beijing.

Sitting on the patio of a trendy restaurant with a steady stream of passing pedestrians is an ideal way to show off new clothes and new friends.

In these modern, often playful environments, young Chinese can laugh, flirt, or just lounge. In a way, they provide the independence and freedom from family supervision that the car represented to American teens in the 20th century. In China, Western-style restaurants provide a haven for young people to socialize and try out their new identities, away from their parents' observant eyes. Ironically, while teens and young adults enjoy the opportunity foreign restaurants provide to relax and socialize away from their parents, they also welcome the public visibility these restaurants afford them. Given the choice, these young customers will choose an outside table, preferably one with a steady stream of pedestrian traffic passing by. Sitting with friends on a restaurant patio or at a hot new club is the ideal way to show off new clothes or even new friends.

For business executives and those who hope to achieve such status, foreign restaurants offer a similar visibility benefit, although in this case, the value is status more than style. Eating at the right foreign restaurant can communicate success and upward mobility. For young families, foreign restaurants provide a new venue for pleasing and entertaining their children. Like their parents before them, these new mothers and fathers associate food with love and are delighted with the new options for expressing it through Happy Meals, themed birthday celebrations, and indoor playgrounds.

Localization: The Fusion of Tastes

The Wal-Mart Supercenter on North Linyi Road in Shanghai is massive even by Wal-mart standards. Its shelves stretch as far as the eye can see, offering a mix of food, appliances, toys, and household goods that make U.S. versions look boring. A shopper can select from countless flavored teas and chips from the U.S., Korea, Japan, or China. Here a young Chinese can shop for frozen dumplings, freshly baked buns, or ready-to-eat vegetable dishes. A shopper can stock up on Western style preserved sausages and ham in the refrigerated section and also visit a "wet market" section that closely resembles traditional Chinese fresh food stands they visited as children. The store sign may say "Wal-Mart," but these stores and other retailers like them are succeeding because of modifications that specifically cater to Chinese customers' desires and behaviors.

This type of modification or localization is rampant in China right now and is largely driven by the tastes and preferences of young urban Chinese. While initially impressed by foreign brands and their non-Chinese qualities, these young consumers have grown more demanding. Now they want both: the new offerings of foreign companies modified to better fit Chinese values and lifestyles. Conversely, they also want traditional Chinese offerings to adopt those desirable traits of imports.

The successful delivery of these hybrids is most evident in the food and restaurant business. The 1200 KFC outlets offer egg rolls and seasonal Chinese vegetables in addition to the fried chicken and biscuits normally on its menu. Häagen-Dazs sells ice cream moon cakes in flavors like passion fruit, beautifully packaged in bright red and gold bags. During the country's annual Spring Festival, McDonald's decorates its golden arches with traditional Chinese decor. Japanese hotpot restaurants offer cooking methods (shabu shabu and teppanyaki) that are classically Japanese but serve ingredients that are all very Chinese.

Li Hua Min drops a bag of Lay's Thai Chicken chips into his backpack as he rushes out the door to meet a friend downtown. On his way, he stops into a KFC and tries their new egg rolls. He meets an old girlfriend for lunch at Yong He Da Wang, a Taiwanese chain famous for its soy milk drinks and dumplings. Like Western-style restaurants, it is spotless and has excellent customer service. Later in the day, Hua Min meets his new girlfriend, an American, at Starbucks. (She seems disappointed that the "venti" size is smaller than she gets in the U.S.) After a long day of socializing and an even longer evening of partying, Hua Min meets some friends at a newly opened Irish pub for some late night karaoke. The music, drinks, and singing fuse together into yet another great night out. Hua Min smiles to himself, feeling fortunate. He is very lucky. Everyone wants to please the Chinese.

Smart grocers like Wal-Mart modify their products and presentation in order to better suit Chinese shoppers' preferences.

Similarly, Yong He Da Wang, the Taiwanese competitor to McDonald's and Burger King, serves familiar Chinese foods in a clean, Western-style fast-food environment. The charmingly named chain, Small Fat Sheep, also offers traditional hotpot meals but in a more contemporary setting. Chatea serves individual portions of Chinese dishes instead of the more traditional communal dishes. In a move echoing Western influences, progressive Chinese or Asian restaurants operate "open" kitchens, exposing the cooking area to their patrons. At BreadTalk, a bakery franchise from Singapore, passers-by can look through a large glass pane and watch pastry chefs as they fill freshly baked buns with cream custards. In another restaurant, customers watch shower-capped staff using bamboo steamers to prepare fresh dumplings.

An even more intriguing take on localization is the fusion of regional Chinese cuisines. For example, Cantonese hotpots typically provide diners with a clear broth and numerous vegetable side dishes to cook in the broth, where Sichuanese hotpots have a spicy soup base focused on meat. Some new restaurants fuse these two cuisines letting customers choose from a variety of hotpot stocks and a wide array of side dishes, including cuts of meats, vegetables and wontons. Ironically, just as regional ingredients and dishes mesh together to form new offerings, some restaurants go in the opposite direction and tease out sub-regional specialties. For example, Shanghai food used to be an "umbrella" cuisine, but now diners can find local Shanghai dishes, Hangzhou dishes, and Suzhou dishes, each cuisine offering a subtle distinction.

While emphasis on localization and fusion currently key in on regional preferences, a likely future scenario is one in which food products become more tailored to particular lifestyles. Evidence of this nascent trend is peeking around the corner. New packaged milk incorporates an ingredient to encourage sleep. A chocolate mix caters to the "on the go" crowd, and a line of flavored water offers to help with relaxation, cleansing, or vitality. These products reflect the recognition that young urban Chinese may not always be satisfied with "new," "imported," or "convenient." Soon food may also need to be "especially for you."

Some new hotpot restaurants fuse different regional cuisines and practices, letting customers choose from a variety of stocks and an array of side dishes.

KFC offers Chinese patrons their version of Chinese spring rollls and seasonal Chinese vegetables in addition to its more traditional fried chicken and biscuits.

Yong He Da Wang is a Taiwanese restaurant that serves Chinese food in a clean, Western-style fast-food environment, complete with a company icon that looks remarkably similar to KFC's Colonel.

7

Zhu (living)

住

住

Although *Zhu* typically refers to housing or residence, we've taken the liberty of expanding it to include the broader concept of home life and leisure time. The idea of a home as a retreat where a person can relax, unwind, and enjoy entertainment at leisure is relatively novel in China. Under Communism, a person's time was directly tied to his or her role in society, and activities that did not contribute to nation building were regarded as unproductive. Mao's brand of socialism essentially erased the boundaries between the personal and the political. The state played a very direct role in dictating how people should lead their private lives: the style of marriage ceremonies, the naming of children, and the décor of homes should ideally reflect the values of communist society. For example, a portrait of Mao adorned every living room, and all signs of any former tendencies, such as non-socialist artwork, religious artifacts, and music that celebrated life before Mao were strictly banned. Leisure pursuits, such as music and theatre, also needed to reflect socialist themes; hence, the Chinese operas depicting Mao's victorious life.

Since the economic reforms initiated in 1979, home life and leisure time in China have gradually moved out of state influence and into individual control. This governmental change is having a dramatic social impact. Rather than being basic shelters, homes and flats are becoming yet another venue for exploring individualism and expressing personality. Bare concrete walls are being covered with modern prints, bright paint, and memorabilia from recent travels. PCs are joining refrigerators and washers as common household appliances linking individual homes to the global Internet as well as to local networks of friends and family. Content streams in from all points of the world to televisions, DVD players, stereos, video game consoles, and even mobile phones. As a result, young urban Chinese are finding it progressively easier to satisfy their passion for personal expression and entertainment during their newfound leisure time.

New and Improved

Until very recently, all dwellings in China were state-owned property. Residents could not buy or sell their homes. As a result, they had little incentive to make improvements, and even if they did, financial resources were limited. Homes were simple, functional shelters rather than an extension of private life. More often than not, several related families lived together sharing costs and space.

Beginning in the early 1990's, the government transitioned away from being the world's largest landlord by privatizing homes and making mortgage loans available. In the wake of these changes, China has experienced a surge in homeownership and suburban expansion reminiscent in many ways of the U.S. housing boom of the 1950s and 1960s. As in the U.S., new housing tracts in China are springing up seemingly overnight where fields and farms once lay. Some of this boom is due to speculators, but the majority of units are bought by families willing to move further from city centers in an effort to get more for their money.

This transition to the suburbs often breaks up the extended families that have lived together for generations. In Chinese, the word *jia* connotes both home and family. Traditionally, home was a place where multiple generations lived under one roof. Once a

Wang Liang and his fiancée walk slowly along the path that snakes through all the levels of the IKEA store on Shanghai's Cao Xi Road. Almost every weekend, they visit a furniture or appliance store, studying the displays for ideas on how to decorate their new home once they are married. When everything is in place, they'll invite their family and friends to come and admire the modern lifestyle they are building. But today, Liang is just buying a new desk for his home computer, and his fiancée has found a brightly colored chair pad for 10 Yuan ($1.25 U.S). They pay for their purchases and take them to the sidewalk in front of the store, where a line of taxi vans wait to cart shoppers back to their homes or flats with their large loads. Someday soon, muses Liang, they will need to use one of the larger vans that can accommodate couches, beds, and cabinets.

woman married, she became part of her husband's *jia* and moved in with his extended family. While it is still common to see extended families living under one roof, young couples with sufficient income to do so now often choose to live independently in their own flat without parents or grandparents.

China's housing boom may be similar to the post-World War II housing boom in the U.S., but the housing stock is not comparable to the large ranch-style homes that came to represent American suburban life. An average flat in one of China's coastal province suburbs is much smaller, averaging between 500 and 1,000 square feet. Freestanding homes with private yards are rare; instead, most new residences are a unit within a high-rise complex built around a small, shared common area. The status and prestige of the complex can be judged by the size and intricacy of its

A two-bedroom flat in this new suburban complex about 45 minutes from Shanghai measures approximately 900 square feet and costs 800,000 Yuan (roughly $100,000 U.S.) which makes it affordable to China's middle-class.

columns, facades, gates, and other details of exterior décor. Also unlike housing in the U.S., a unit is sold as an empty concrete shell—with bare walls and no lighting, flooring, or appliances. Seeing it as a finished home takes imagination and the help of China's rapidly growing home-furnishing industry.

Home developers sell units as concrete shells, without flooring, lighting, or any appliances.

The spike in home ownership and the need to decorate and furnish units from the bare walls has been the catalyst behind the growth of China's home-improvement market, which the consulting firm Bain & Co. recently estimated at $15 billion in sales, growing at 10 percent. Rather than saving money to start a family as their parents may have done, many young urban couples have shifted their priorities to making a home that's unique and reflects their lifestyle.

As with fashion, a typical approach to buying home furnishing starts with a trip to a Western store which may be too high priced but provides inspiration. We accompanied one young couple as they visited a chic new furniture store in Shanghai. They visited the location for ideas, closely examining the design of pieces they liked and measuring their dimensions. They then took the measurements and design details to a local woodworking shop that custom-made the furniture for them at a much lower price. Another couple marrying in the fall and planning for their new home explained to us that they will buy from IKEA. They conceded that IKEA furniture may not be sturdy enough to last very long, but they like the look of the store's "cool" and modern furniture. Since they plan to change and update their decor frequently, the lower quality doesn't bother them.

As these young couples rush to fill their homes with symbols of modern living, appliances and electronics are also enjoying record sales. This latest wave of refrigerators, washers and ranges

Young Chinese are attracted to window-shopping at stores like Simply Life that inspire them with modern, expensive furnishings.

come in a wide variety of sizes, shapes, and colors, a stark contrast to the generic designs of past decades when appliances were made by state-owned companies. Status features, such as a wine-storage compartment on a refrigerator door, are becoming commonplace.

Those looking for more than inspiration visit stores like IKEA, Gome, Yongle or Suning where they can buy more affordably priced goods

Consumers can now shop for appliances that come in more sizes, styles and colors than when they were manufactured and sold by state-owned entities.

This storage compartment on the door of a refrigerator indicates that its owner can afford and appreciates wine, a relatively new beverage in China.

Shopping in stores that display an international aesthetic and lifestyle gives these consumers a sense that their living conditions and design choices are on par with the rest of the developed world. Unlike their U.S. counterparts, however, Chinese consumers overwhelmingly pay cash for their purchases and are not living lifestyles based on easy credit. According to the *China Business Weekly,* only 2 million Chinese hold credit cards, a condition that is unlikely to expand quickly because the government retains control of the financial system and lacks the infrastructure to create or maintain a large credit operation. However, private creditors are cautiously optimistic about the future of plastic money in China

Credit remains relatively scarce in China. Most household purchases are still made in cash, which limits purchasing power compared to more credit dependent economies in the West.

as they see the government taking its first steps in this direction, such as the recent establishment of the Consumer Credit Bureau. If young Chinese show a willingness to use credit wisely, this trend will likely accelerate.

The media tends to spotlight the explosion of suburban living, but not all young Chinese are suburbanites. The cost of home ownership and the long commute put too great a burden on those building their careers and enjoying an active social life; living in or near the city center keeps them close to work and the entertain- ment meccas they frequent on weekends. Particularly for singles, renting a downtown flat is often a more attractive and affordable option than buying a home in the suburbs. To this group, the suburbs represent boredom. One young woman we recently interviewed was distraught over her company's plans to relocate to Pudong, a suburb of Shanghai. Although she could afford a larger flat after the move, she agonized over what her daily life would lose, including proximity to hundreds of good restaurants and fashionable shops.

Since young singles spend so little time at home, most down- town flats are barely more than dorm rooms, typically shared with others. Gaining status through the look of their home is not likely at this stage in their lives, and they would rather spend their money improving their public image than buying, decorating and maintaining a home. They move frequently, so they avoid bulky or big-ticket items and instead use minor accessories to inject personal taste. It takes much less money to impress others with new makeup, clothes, or the latest mobile phone.

Young Chinese who want to be close to shopping and entertainment often choose to live in large dorms or apartment complexes common in the urban centers of China's largest cities.

Chen Hong carefully listens to a dozen different songs before choosing the perfect back-ground music for her website on Fzone.cn. She has worked for weeks to design a site that reflects her personality and expresses all of her interests. It has pictures of her in her many different moods, as well as shots of her friends and the celebrities she adores. She's chosen cute cartoon animations to decorate the photos, and she loves the virtual bedroom she's deco-rated in pink and blue. She writes in her online journal everyday, using tiny icons to let her readers know her emotional state. Dozens of her friends are online right now, so she takes a break from designing to chat with some of them and share a new music clip a Korean friend sent her. Maybe in exchange someone will send her a new animation to add to her collection. Hong jokes that she owns more virtual objects than real ones.

Living Online

For a young person whose living space is the size of a large walk-in closet and shared with parents or roommates, the online world represents the ultimate in freedom and privacy. Particularly for young urbanites, the introduction of the Internet to China has been nothing short of revolutionary. Before the 1990s, access to communication technology was limited, and few could afford even landlines. Newspapers and media tended to focus on officially acceptable stories, giving little perspective onto what everyday people thought and did. With the Internet, young Chinese are now able to create new social worlds for leisure, information seek-ing, entertainment, and networking. Despite the government's attempt to maintain censorship, wired citizens are able to con-nect with people from around the world and discuss new ideas, philosophies, and beliefs. The Internet provides them with a virtual soapbox, a stage where they can express thoughts and opinions publicly that previously were forbidden. In addition, it's an enor-mous resource of shared music, videos, movies, games, books, and timesaving tools—all available at the end of a quick search.

Mainland China has 111 million Internet users according to a government survey in April 2006, 64 million of these users have broadband access. Although this is slightly less than 10 percent of the population, it is enough to make China the second largest online population, exceeded only by the U.S. If we consider only users under 30, then China's 79 million young digerati are already the largest online youth group in the world. The majority connect from home, but at least 30 million go online from China's 265,000 Internet cafes, where high-speed access costs 2 to 6 yuan per hour (25 to 75 cents).

Regardless of how or where they connect, these young users are entranced by the possibilities the Internet brings, particularly its ability to support their desire to socialize and their longing for personal expression. Instant messaging, email, and even video connections like that provided by Skype link old friends and new

Over 70 percent of mainland China's 111 million computer users connect from home.

Internet Usage and Behavior — China vs. US

Users	US[1]	China[2]
Internet users	147 million[3]	111 million
% of population	73%	9%
Internet usage — location		
At home	66%	71%
At work	62%	38%
Internet cafes	NA	27%
Public place (via mobile devices)	9%	1%
Mobile phone/internet comparison [4]		
% PCs per HH	72%	17%
Mobile phone user penetration (%)	66%	39%
Mobile phone/internet user ratio	1.2	5.2
Online services used		
Email	91%	91%
News	68%	79%
Search (Web surfing or browsing)	91%	65%
Music downloads	25%	46%
TV & Movies	42%	38%
Games	31%	23%
IM	39%	42%
Shopping	52%	26%[5]

[1] China Internet Network Information Center (CNNIC), 17th Statistical Survey Report on the Internet Development of China, January 2006
[2] China Internet Network Information Center (CNNIC), 17th Statistical Survey Report on the Internet Development of China, January 2006
[3] Pew Internet & American Life Survey, April 2006
[4] Pyramid Data Reports, 2006
[5] China Internet Network Information Center (CNNIC), China Online Shopping Market Survey Report, May 2006

Approximately 30 million young people access the Internet through China's 265,000 Internet cafes. A typical cafe seats 60 to 120 patrons; larger ones can have 500 or more seats.

acquaintances through a PC or mobile phone. Bulletin boards, discussion groups and social networks like Fzone.cn, Lianqu.com. cn, and MSN Spaces provide an unlimited, constantly changing stage on which young Chinese can perform. One young woman's blog on Fzone.cn for example, talks about her appreciation for life, explaining how happy she is to have her basic needs met, to be able to listen to music, and to have people who love her. Another young man poetically describes his feelings towards love by posting "Love is like drinking coffee. The aroma smells so good and tempting, but when you drink it, it's bitter."

Some commentators believe that this adoption of the Internet represents the rise of a true civil society in China, one in which people can engage in open debate about philosophy and values. If so, it's taking off quickly. At last count, 60 million Chinese—more than one half of the online population—were posting blogs. The mere idea that a person could publicly state his or her opinion about anything—life, love, or even weather—is extraordinary to the average Chinese and is creating a nation of young bloggers. Although the government maintains a sizeable force dedicated to keeping Internet discussions and information within prescribed boundaries, users are rapidly finding ways to get around the restrictions. Satiric blogs that are thinly veiled political statements are becoming more prominent.

For most users, the connections these sites and applications facilitate become like extended family—a support system that is a natural expansion of Chinese networking practices. Sites that link people of the same college, hometown, and other leisure interests are proliferating as they provide a place for young Chinese to meet others and ultimately create communities. Even online dating is taking off. Baihe, which claims to be China's largest online dating site, attracted more than 5 million users in 2005, according to iResearch Consulting Group in China. Behavior on these dating sites reflects the growing interest among young Chinese to find romantic love and to buck the tradition of arranged marriages. The online activities young people pursue and the more explicit language they use in their search for casual encounters indicate a loosening of social mores relating to sexuality.

As much as social connection drives much of China's online traffic, so does the allure of entertainment, especially online gaming. According to a recent market intelligence report from In-stat, online gamers in China will grow from 25.5 million in 2005 to 61 million in 2010. Currently, most are young men engaged in "massively multiplayer online role-playing games," or MMORPGs, in which players assume the roles of fictional characters within the confines of a created online environment and engage with competitors in battles, quests, and other activities. Popular titles tend to come from Korea and Japan, but local Chinese games are catching on, particularly those based on martial arts novels, historical legends, and famous wars.

MMORPGs allow friends to talk and socialize even while they play from separate locations. As such, they recreate the camaraderie players often experienced in Internet cafes. This may explain how players can spend an average of 3 to 4 hours in these virtual roles per day.

Sites like Fzone.cn, which are similar to MySpace and BeBo in the U.S., attract millions of young Chinese bloggers who quickly learn to use the sites' advanced customizing features and push the companies to offer more.

Online language and behaviors offer visible proof of changing beliefs and practices that may be more hidden offline.

Entertain Me

Li Hua Min saunters into his favorite Internet café and checks with his friend who manages the shop during the day. Today is slow—only 400 users online—but it will get more crowded as the day progresses and the younger game-playing boys arrive. The government says a person must be 18 to log on in this café, but everyone ignores this restriction. Hua Min finds an open chair and uses his debit card to initiate a session. He's hung over from partying late last night, so he avoids anything that requires thinking. Instead, he dons the headphones and starts to search for new videos to download and watch. He reminds himself to check Taobao to find one of the new phones that play movies.

Home entertainment in the U.S. has expanded to take over entire living rooms, parts of kitchens, and in the case of new homes, even some bathrooms. China's appetite for entertainment is no less than the U.S., but the small size of Chinese homes or apartments limits the option in home entertainment. Rarely is a home in China large enough to regularly entertain friends. Although some find a way to install full home theatre setups or large dining tables, most cannot accommodate the spacious entertainment set ups common in the U.S. As a result, much leisure time entertainment is self focused, portable, and intended to relax or amuse just one or two people.

American entertainment media has some presence in China, but Korean media is far more popular. Korean movies, dramas and pop music are in extremely high demand; in fact, in 2002 a total of 67 South Korean television shows debuted on screens nationwide. "Winter Sonata" and "Jewel of Palace" have been two of the most popular. The former is credited with sparking the "*han liu*" or Korean Wave phenomena in China, and the latter one reached an all-time high audience penetration of nearly 10 percent. Korean stars often become major celebrities in China. Images and photos of 23 year-old Rain, the reigning Korean pop star, decorate notebooks, mobile phone covers, backpacks, and computer desktop screens for millions of adoring Chinese fans.

By Western standards, many of the shows in China seem nostalgic and dated, but the underlying technology certainly is not. Ten years ago China had only two television channels, both state-owned. Now there are dozens, including CNN and MTV. Several stations broadcast to PCs over the Internet. Shows encourage audiences to determine winners by casting votes via SMS on their cell phones, as millions did to determine the winner of the Super Girl Voice show in 2005, a competition similar to American Idol that over 20 million Chinese viewers regularly watched. Those who can afford it download shows and movies to watch on their mobile phones. Those on more restricted budgets can purchase popular TV shows and movies on DVD from thousands of street vendors for 8 to 10 yuan (about $1 U.S.).

If movies on DVD are cheap in China, music is even cheaper. In fact, for most young urban Chinese it is nearly free, courtesy of music-sharing sites on the Internet and pirated CDs that hit the streets almost as soon as a legitimate CD is released. As with broadcast media, Korean artists reign supreme today, but some Westerners and a few Chinese performers are popular as well. For example, singers from Hong Kong such as Andy Lau, Karen Mok, and Shelly Chen have recorded songs in Mandarin to cater specifically toward the vast Chinese market.

Music and film are closely linked in China, with movie stars often becoming singers and singers becoming movie stars. Young Chinese tend to prefer soft pop, rock, or less frequently, hip-hop. Chinese in the Southern provinces enjoy "Canto-pop," a style of song and celebrity that comes primarily from Hong Kong. Hits are usually highly commercialized, with the music packaged in combination with the celebrity status of its performers, and as part of its promotion immediately released to the wildly popular karaoke bars. China's music channels present new acts and chart toppers continuously. Usually these performers sing, but they may also dance, talk, act, or just giggle and smile. Music is gradually becoming an expression of individualism. While new acts are likely to copy others rather than break new ground, there is a growing number of artists who are striving to express their opinions through music.

Popular movies and music garner much attention because of the new growth areas that they represent within China, but while digital and broadcast media has exploded in recent years, reading material has always been popular. China has a huge audience of readers accustomed to paying 15 to 20 yuan ($2 to $3 U.S.) for a book. Bookstores in major urban centers are often larger than most U.S. department stores, and entire floors may be devoted to specific genres, ranging from classical Chinese fiction to advanced computer-programming tutorials. The Chinese government also uses books as an efficient means of disseminating

Young Chinese have been able to watch movies or TV dramas at home for over a decade. What's new is being able to use DVRs to time-shift programs for greater convenience and accessing satellite broadcasts.

The ready availability of video content has left theatres largely vacant and movie retail shops gathering dust on their inventory.

information, such as recent publications that explain the history of the Olympics and its proceedings. In a recent visit, we even found Internet content that had been printed out and bound in book form.

Young Chinese may be pressed for time, but they nevertheless are trying to absorb as much information about the world around them as they can. Like new restaurants and foreign shopping centers, translated publications give readers a taste of how others live. Chinese versions of the Harry Potter series have appeared on bookstore shelves within days of its English version release, and they are snapped up by fans who are fascinated to read books that capture the world's attention. The sign "banned publications from China" is prominently displayed in airport bookstores in Hong Kong to attract Chinese travelers searching for information wherever it can be found, even if acquiring it is technically illegal.

With their busy schedules some young Chinese are finding less time to read books and newspapers, but magazines are easy to consume and more new titles are available each month. China has its own version of *Reader's Digest,* called *Reader*, which attracts a young audience with its presentation of cultural values and positive editorial content. But young urban Chinese are increasingly gravitating toward lifestyle magazines, particularly those with attractive visuals.

Influenced by Japan, much of the content of fashion and home life magazines is instructional—teaching readers how to decorate rooms, wear new styles, and refine their make-up. One recent article tells readers how to manage space at home more efficiently by using vertical cabinets, and to use mirrors or lights to increase overall space. Do-it-yourself columns are proliferating in both home décor and fashion magazines. Men's magazines are also finding new readers, as are local Chinese editions of inter-national periodicals like *Vogue* and *Marie Claire,* which introduce their readers to even more elaborate notions of the good life.

Books and periodicals on almost any topic are available in China's enormous multi-floor bookstores.

Dozens of young celebrities smile from the covers of popular fashion magazines

8

Xing (mobility)

行

行

Xing conveys two meanings. The more traditional is *transport*, or the simple process of getting from point A to point B. A more modern connotation includes the sense of *freedom* young Chinese urbanites are discovering as they create personal, private space yet remain connected to others; as they explore and develop new social communities while maintaining strong ties with their parents; and as they learn to move more freely around a country the size of the U.S. and a world they were previously forbidden to visit.

To the generation now coming of age in China, both aspects of mobility—transport and freedom—are critically important and intertwined. For them, mobility is a lifestyle, complete with its own fashions and status symbols. It revolves around autos and other means of travel but also includes the one device that the mobile crowd finds most indispensable—the mobile phone. As this lifestyle grows and expands over the coming decades, it seems certain that any products, services, and industries even remotely related to mobility will skyrocket.

From Bikes to Cars

Visit any city in China, even the more sophisticated coastal cities, and you see that "sea of bicycles" is more than a metaphor. It's unlikely anyone has made an accurate count, but if we assume everyone old enough or young enough to ride a bike has one, a billion would be a reasonable guess. For over a century, one-speed bikes have been the main transportation mode for the majority of Chinese. Even as recently as 1990, bicyles dominated Beijing's main throughways. In all but the largest cities, bikes remain the most common form of transportation: they carry students to school, workers to their jobs, and couriers to their deliveries' destinations.

In comparison, China has only about 15.5 million automobiles, or 1.2 cars per 100 people. In a country with well over a billion in population, this is a relatively low level of penetration, yet China is the world's third-largest consumer of automobiles, and climbing at a speedy clip. In 2005, Chinese purchased approximately 2.3 million cars, and a McKinsey report predicts a 20 percent annual increase in passenger car sales through 2007. In the past, most cars in China were bought by governmental institutions and companies, but now the majority is being purchased by individuals. Ask young Chinese what they dream and you're likely to hear it is to own a car. To them, owning a car is a sure sign of success and a highly visible symbol of modern living, particularly if they live in the suburbs.

More than 50 brands compete for this business, including companies from Japan, Europe, the United States, and Korea. Their offerings range from low-cost basic compacts to top-of-the line luxury sedans, usually marketed as a joint venture with a Chinese company to meet government regulations. Currently, the market is fragmented by popular foreign brands, including Audi, BMW, Mercedes-Benz, Buick, Honda, and Volkswagen. Chery Automotive has become the leading local brand (and, yes, the company's name is remarkably similar to Chevy).

Wang Liang has been to the Shanghai International Raceway three times. The first time he went, right after it opened in 2004, he had been one of the few lucky recipients of tickets from his company. Since then, he's eagerly awaited the upcoming races and paid the admission himself. The thrill of seeing of a Ferrari or a Porsche going by at nearly 200 kilometers per hour makes him yearn for one of his own. Liang knows in reality he'll probably never be able to own either car, but the opportunity to see, touch, even sit in one without a dealer pressuring him is an experience he can't pass up. When the Shanghai Auto Show is in town, Liang and his friends, armed with their digital cameras, always make it a day's event. They are captivated by the latest styles, not to mention the beautiful women showcasing the cars. His photo collection of Mercedes and BMW automobiles contains hundreds of shots, and he proudly posts the best ones on his website.

Cyclists swarm through the busy streets of China's cities, mingling comfortably with cars, cabs, motorcycles, and buses. Oftentimes, a tight row of two dozen riders or more will snake through the city together.

Despite these early leads, no one yet has a lock on this market. Brand awareness is low, and consumers are still forming perceptions of cars and the people who drive them.

Most Chinese car owners are first- or second-time buyers with only a few years of exposure to influence their impressions of brands. As competitors scramble to gain share in what all expect will soon be the world's largest automobile market, they are marketing aggressively and dropping prices—all of which complicates brand attachment. In fact, according to a 2005 report from Mercer management consulting, "Chinese Automotive Market 2010," only 25 percent of car owners in China choose the same brand when they buy their next car, compared to almost 80 percent loyalty in Western industrial countries.

At an average price of 160,000 yuan ($20,000 U.S.), a car is likely the first, and possibly only, major purchase for young, urban Chinese until they purchase a home. Most choose locally made, mid-level foreign cars, which offer a combination of better quality assurance, high status, and affordability. A luxury brand like BMW is highly desirable but unattainable for most, so to create the allure of status, some car makers have added luxury symbolism

Most Chinese car owners are first- or second-time buyers, with little experience in the process and few established brand perceptions.

to mid-level cars. Both the Toyota Camry and GM's Buick have upright medallions on their hoods similar to the classic icons of BMW and Mercedes.

Some buyers will forgo luxury status and choose a lower-priced car whose brand, styling, or color better reflects their lifestyle. Cars like the Volkswagen Polo and the Chery QQ are good examples. The neon-colored subcompacts dot the streets of China's major cities. Their bright visibility conveys a sense of personality and youthful individualism that blander models lack. Modifications to Western models also reflect a sense of Chinese culture and beliefs. Unlike the Polo's European cousin, most models in China are not hatchbacks. To most Chinese, a hatch-back car is incomplete because the "tail" has been chopped off—and that's unlucky.

Auto advertising will certainly heat up in the coming years, but right now, the most pervasive influence on car buyers is what they see on the streets of cities like Beijing, Shanghai, and Guangzhou. Car shows, websites, celebrities, and advertising add detail and

Brightly colored subcompacts can be seen darting in and out of traffic throughout China's major cities.

For those Chinese with more disposable income, cars can be personalized with custom detailing.

endorsement, but the most persuasive of all is the example of other Chinese who can already afford to own a car. Seeing the colorful Polo all over town or the upscale Audi parked in front of prestigious addresses tells young Chinese that these are the most desirable cars because their wealthier compatriots are buying them.

World Travelers

By 2020, the World Trade Organization estimates, 100 million Chinese will travel overseas every year. In slightly more than a decade, China will have gone from being a nation of cloistered citizens to being the world's largest source of outbound tourists. Rising incomes and relaxed travel regulations are significant drivers of this outward flow, but the rise of a young, more worldly and experimental generation is arguably the strongest force. As one young Chinese women explained, even though people of her parents' generation have saved sufficient money to travel the world, most have no desire to leave China. She and her friends, on the other hand, are ready to pack their bags at a moment's notice.

For now, favorite destinations for these newest globetrotters remain close to home. Destinations within China, especially Shanghai and Beijing, top the list of most young travelers, particularly those visiting from smaller, less developed cities. During a recent trip to Beijing, we saw flocks of Chinese tourists at the Forbidden City, each group identified by a cap of a different color. As they pointed to artifacts and talked among themselves, we heard every possible Chinese dialect.

Hong Kong has been attracting sizeable contingents of mainland Chinese tourists, many seeking more authentic and less expensive goods than those available on the mainland. The Chinese government actually encourages this exchange by allowing citizens of selected cities such as Guangzhou, Shanghai, and Beijing to travel independently to Hong Kong, rather than requiring that they go with a group. To accommodate these new tourists, Hong Kong has needed to make changes. Mainland Chinese tourists want decent accommodations but prefer to reserve most of their travel money for presents, so Hong Kong has created more two- and three-star hotels, which don't emphasize luxury. Tourists from Shanghai and Beijing don't speak Cantonese, which is favored in Hong Kong, so local shopkeepers are becoming more adept at Mandarin.

Not all domestic tourism is focused on big cities and shopping centers. More and more Chinese are expressing their love for their country's beauty and history by vacationing to local points of interest in less developed areas. UNESCO and the Chinese government have made significant progress in establishing World Heritage Sites, including obvious choices like the Great Wall, Yellow Mountains (Huangshan), and the Summer Palace in Beijing, as well as lesser-known places such as the ancient villages of Xidi and Hongcun. We've frequently encountered young couples or groups of students traveling together in China's rural provinces. We even come across small groups of college-aged young girls traveling on their own.

Chen Hong clicks through dozens of webpages each night, planning her next vacation. Last year she visited Shanghai with a tour group of other young Chinese. This year, Hong has decided to do something more adventurous by traveling to a foreign country. She is going to visit the location of her favorite Korean soap opera, "Jewel of the Palace." As part of one tour package she's considering, Hong would experience the same exciting food, events, and scenes as she sees on the show. According to the tour operator, Hong would even be able to pose as the leading lady—dressing in her costumes and wearing her makeup! Sitting back in her chair, Hong reflects on this part of her education: visiting other cultures is the perfect way to learn about the world, but actually living like others— particularly a famous actress— is even better.

Digital cameras help young Chinese capture memories of their travel to post on their websites or share with friends. Because travel is still relatively rare and intermittent, travel photos are a precious reminder of the experience.

Chinese prefer to stay in more modest two- or three-star hotels, saving their money for luxury goods and travel experiences. What a Chinese tourist can save on hotels she might splurge on the latest Louis Vuitton bag.

Outside of China, other Asian, American, and European destinations appeal to young travelers interested in gaining a broader view of the world. Japan, Vietnam, South Korea, Thailand, the U.S., and the raft of European nations that recently earned authorized destination status (ADS) from the Chinese government are all attractive to pioneering groups of tourists. Generally, these travelers prefer to stay in modest hotels and spend their days sightseeing, going to theme parks, dining out, and visiting karaoke bars. For these types of trips, most Chinese feel more comfortable traveling with a group, on a fixed agenda led by a tour guide. The kind of post-college backpacker who travels with a Lonely Planet guidebook and a couple of pairs of underwear is not a popular model for Chinese. Nor is the traveler who only stays in five-star hotels and eats according to the critics' ratings. But it's reasonable to predict that both of these extremes will include future Chinese travelers. As tourism and travel soar, the diversity and appetite of Chinese travelers will expand as well.

While Beijing, Shanghai, and Hong Kong are popular destinations for young Chinese, more adventurous travelers head to rural locations. These art students from Guangzhou are sketching buildings in the ancient town of Hongcun.

Li Hua Min walks down a drab hallway into the noisy, crowded mobile phone store that showcases all the latest goods of the top brands. The minute he walks through the door, a dozen young sales associates start shouting at him to look at the new models they have, but Hua Min can't be seduced by their tactics. He's checked out all of the top models online and knows exactly how their features compare. His choice will definitely be a foreign brand; Chinese brands have no image yet. He doesn't really worry about voice quality because he rarely uses his phone to talk with people, but it must be easy to text-message. The camera and MP3 player should have a simple interface, and the video quality should be good enough for viewing downloadable movies. Of course he will use his phone to connect to the Internet and download games, so the screen size is important. Hua Min is confident he can find a lower price through eBay or Taobao, but before he buys, he needs to touch the handset and see how it feels. That's still something you can't do online.

In the coming decade the Chinese are expected to surpass the U.S. to become the world's second-largest consumer of luxury goods (behind Japan), much of it purchased while abroad. Even travelers with relatively modest means will allocate a large slice for luxury purchases, unlike most of their fellow guests at Motel 6 and Budget Inn. For Chinese travelers, the goal is not just to bring back trinkets or common souvenirs from abroad, but also to bring back items for friends and extended family that are hard to obtain, expensive, or have famous labels.

Mobile but Connected

If being mobile is a goal, then staying connected while mobile is a prerequisite, particularly for China's urban teens and young adults who consider mobile phones as symbols of their new social freedom. The number of users rises daily as more Chinese buy their first mobile phone, but as of June 2005, the Chinese government tagged it at 380 million, projecting a climb to over 440 million by 2007. Even if every man, woman and child in the U.S. and Canada had a mobile phone, they would not equal China's current population of users.

The phones and the connections they facilitate are a microcosm of the expanding desires of two types of users: those who use mobile phones primarily for social and entertainment reasons, and those who use them more for business or productivity reasons. Users motivated by social or entertainment needs drive demand for MP3 players, which saw a growth of over 100 percent in 2005. They also include a sizeable audience of mobile game players, predominately young men, who download games from Internet portals of China's ISPs, such as China Mobile. Purchasers whose main priority is business productivity, rather than entertainment, want all the capabilities of PCs, including email, date and contact management, productivity applications, and support for multilingual and multicultural contexts, along with voice communication for business calls.

*Young urban Chinese wouldn't think of
leaving their mobile phones behind.*

*A text message costs about .1 Yuan to send (less
and one-quarter of a U.S. cent), which the majority
of the young urban population can easily afford.*

*For many young users, their mobile phones are a
fashion accessory that they proudly display.*

*Business users may rely on their mobile
phone for most of the features and capabilities
associated with PCs.*

Both types of mobile phone subscribers keep in touch with peers primarily by SMS, a very cheap form of text messaging, and the number of messages this use generates is staggering. In 2005, somewhere between 250 to 300 billion instant text messages were sent by Chinese mobile phones, up from less than 2 billion in 2001. In 2005, Beijing Mobile handled more than one billion outgoing short messages sent between family members on Lunar New Year's Eve alone. Considering China's ideograph-based written language includes 50,000 characters, it's a marvel that these messages could be composed, let alone sent. Most young Chinese can comfortably and quickly use a mix of Pinyin Chinese characters, numbers, and English in their text and email messages. As in the U.S. and elsewhere, heavy users adopt SMS slang.

Those with more social reasons for their mobile phones may subscribe to services that send jokes, stories, or news via SMS, or they may subscribe to news on fashion, pop culture, or music. A busy entrepreneur might use text messaging to confirm the location of a meeting or to let a client know he's running late. Technologies such as SMS have also been a powerful way to spread news rapidly throughout China. During the recent SARS epidemic, people used SMS to communicate to each other what news they had.

Mobile phones outnumber PCs in China, and because they serve many as their main access to the Internet, there is an enormous market for mobile content services of all types—online dating, blogging, language courses, and more. These services are contracted out to Internet portal companies such as Netease, Sina,

Websites hawk the latest downloadable games for mobile phones. Some are free, the rest cost an average of 5 to 6 yuan (75 cents U.S.).

Sohu, and Tom, which use the ISP's billing platforms to allow consumers to buy over the Internet. Purchases are added to their monthly phone bills—a necessary convenience in a country without credit cards.

Beyond their functionality, mobile phones are a status symbol and for many, a fashion statement. Nokia seems to be the top choice for China's trendiest young users who are keenly aware of image, but Korean brands are catching up by offering more creative designs and leveraging their celebrity connections. One young girl explained that she bought her latest phone because her favorite celebrity, Rain, uses the same brand and model. Viewers of the 2004 movie "Cell Phone" couldn't miss the obvious Motorola product placements throughout the movie. But brand image is only the starting point for mobile phones as fashion accessories. Numerous websites offer downloadable ring tones, screen savers, and wallpaper to decorate the phone's interface. Having multiple faceplates in different colors is taken for granted, as is the addition of dangling charms. For more customizing, owners drop their phones off at street stalls to have jeweled designs or personal engravings added.

Although not currently popular with young Chinese, China's domestic mobile phone brands could become formidable global competitors.

All this end-user enthusiasm is fueling a frothy market for manufacturers and investors. According to ARC Group, a leading wireless industry research firm, total mobile entertainment revenues are forecast to grow from $1.1 billion in 2004 to $3.6 billion in 2008, an increase of 37 percent. Domestic Chinese companies like Minren and Hi-Tech Wealth have done well with simple, inexpensive handsets used mainly for voice calls, but young urban consumers want more advanced and upscale hardware. These same users might feel fine about buying Chinese brands for their DVD players, karaoke machines, and other electronics, but they will not yet consider buying a Chinese phone. The desire for more than basic phones and the appeal of Western brands has helped global vendors, notably Nokia, Motorola, and Samsung, dominate in market share, but it's too early to count China's brand out. Given their tough training ground, a few years from now they may be competitive not only in China, but on a global scale as well.

9

Future Present

One of the most difficult challenges in writing this book has been the frequency with which we've needed to update our data, because China is changing so rapidly and so insistently in every field that by the time you read this book, the numbers will have changed again. It's almost as if China has no present, only the approaching future.

Despite the speed of its approach, some aspects of China's future are reasonably predictable. Barring anomalous events like aliens landing or a cataclysmic earthquake decimating Shanghai, the economy of China should continue to grow at least 6 to 8 percent a year over the next five to ten years, possibly even faster, official government predictions suggest. Continued economic growth should help the middle class continue to expand, and the country overall should become wealthier as a consequence.

While some facets of China's future are predictable, we can't always foresee their impact. For example, more Chinese will surely gain access to the Internet as computers and mobile phones spread throughout the country, but it is difficult to determine with any degree of certainty how this increased knowledge, global contact, and massive interconnectedness will influence Chinese behaviors and attitudes. It may have only moderate impact. The Chinese could integrate all that technology brings and make their current systems and culture work faster, smoother, and more effectively. On the other hand, this kind of connectivity may radically transform the country and its culture by introducing and spreading new philosophies and expectations that gain popular support and prompt widespread change.

Similarly, we can predict that as China's economy grows and expands, its citizens will become more experienced consumers. What we can't foresee is how they will express this new sophistication. Demands for customization and personalization could race well beyond current expectations. Response to advertising could change as the Chinese become more familiar with the global stage and its many celebrities. Their preference in shopping experiences could morph to one that's almost entirely online. The sheer size of the Chinese marketplace will give it the power to dictate terms to marketers and manufacturers, particularly once China's domestic brands start competing on par with other global leaders and the word "imported" loses its magnetic appeal.

And while we can predict some things with confidence and envision other scenarios based on well-founded hypotheses, a significant portion of China's future remains too volatile to even guess. Can a country as vast as China really moderate the flow of its population from rural areas to urban? Can its environment survive its economic growth? Can the government redesign itself to support full participation in a largely capitalist global economy? Can the country remodel its educational system to support an economy that values innovation over conformity? Can the nation of "little emperors" produced by China's one child policy learn the collaboration and leadership skills needed in the workplace? These are questions we debate among ourselves and that we resist offering firm opinions about. As to those prognosticators who claim to have a reliable, detailed map of these parts of China's future, we remain skeptical.

Nevertheless, we can and do offer recommendations to succeed as a brand, business, or professional in China today. The following guidelines are based on our research and experience with its young change agents. We use them ourselves as design principles to ground and focus our efforts and strategies.

Beware of Stereotypes

Myths and stereotypes about the Chinese abound in the press, in marketing books, and in presentations. One of the most prevalent false characterizations is that the Chinese are a homogenous people. The fact is that China is a multicultural country that recognizes 56 nationalities within its borders. Ethnic groups often cluster in geographic areas, contributing to notable regional distinctions. The great majority of the Chinese population (92 percent) is Han, but this group subdivides into many distinct groups with significant linguistic, social, and cultural differences. As individuals stream into the large metropolitan areas from all points of China, they bring their ethnic and regional differences with them, contributing to the mix of influences brewing in Beijing, Shanghai, Guangzhou, and their sister cities along the coast.

Another common misconception is that all Chinese are influenced by Confucianism. Confucianism has a long and intimate tie to China and many practitioners among its population, but it is not synonymous with being Chinese. Any business strategy based exclusively on Confucianism will seem naive and irrelevant to many Chinese.

Similarly misguided is the belief that all Chinese adhere to communal values. Among the young middle class, personal independence is increasingly important. Communalism is a strong ethic among many Chinese, but thinking it's their only governing principle is like saying all Americans are only interested in personal independence.

Keep Up with Changes

Don't include an "Enter China" bullet point in your PowerPoint deck unless you're committed to keeping up with massive change. Most businesses are accustomed to markets that change slowly from year to year, or that vary within narrow boundaries; that expectation is dangerous in China, where exponential growth is the norm and where one area routinely influences another. To avoid obsolescence, research conducted to influence decisions in year one must be re-evaluated before using it to guide decisions in years three, four, and five.

Fortunately, China is one of the most thoroughly studied markets in the world, and information about it abounds. Most of the country's leading newspapers, like the *Shanghai Daily* or the *Beijing Daily,* have digital versions available for a small subscription fee. The leading consulting firms issue complimentary newsletters. And don't underestimate the value of bloggers, who track hundreds of different topics and provide firsthand commentary and illustrative photos. Even the Chinese government itself contributes to this flood of intelligence, regularly publishing reports and updates on all aspects of the country's growth.

China has well-developed facilities for gathering input from consumers, business leaders, and average citizens. Most leading research companies have offices in China or established relations with local providers.

Empathize with Consumers

Most companies and institutions understand and declare the importance of connecting with their customers. Understanding the young Chinese consumers represents a particularly intricate challenge, however, because so many of their behaviors and attitudes are in flux. For this reason, we strongly recommend the combination of firsthand experience and longitudinal tracking as the most reliable means of acquiring accurate depth and perspective on the needs and desires of young Chinese.

Secondary sources—this book included—can never fully capture all the nuance and detail needed to refine a specific product or service. Simply knowing or studying Chinese-American culture does not equate to understanding the people of China.

Nothing can substitute for personal, on-site experience. Most of the insights in this book are the result of over ten years of repeat visits to China, followed by regular discussions on the nature of the changes happening there. Some of these trips are quick and focused on a particular objective, but others allow time for more spontaneous interactions. One of the most enjoyable and fruitful evenings Christopher spent on a recent trip to China was when she joined her guide's extended family for dinner in their 300 square-foot flat. Only Gloria, the guide, spoke both Mandarin and English, but throughout the evening everyone from the 11-year-old niece to the grandmother managed to share their thoughts on politics, education, shopping, music, and food.

These types of encounters help us see the world through the eyes and minds of the Chinese and witness for ourselves the changes they are experiencing. These types of visits provide the opportunity to ask unstructured questions, like whom do they admire, how is life changing for them, and what do they dream? The answers to questions like these shed light in unexpected areas and offer an invaluable glimpse of the future direction of the country.

Invest in Meaning

Gone are the days when a company could simply add a few Chinese characters and a dragon to their package and hope to woo millions of buyers. Chinese consumers are rapidly gaining the knowledge and sophistication of consumers in other developed nations and learning to expect more than imagery. As the country continues to grow and prosper, products and services that create experiences and convey relevant meaning will find a hungry market in China.

This is especially true for young Chinese consumers who are growing up with far more abundant choices than their parents. They expect a viable brand to have emotional appeal and clear identity. They will have learned that under capitalism, market competition gives consumers the power to influence the direction that innovation takes. The rise of domestic brands, supported by a homegrown understanding of consumers' culture and values, will raise the bar even higher. A mobile phone that truly embodies the concept of *guanxiwang* (personal support networks) to young Chinese will have a far stronger appeal than one with a cute design, flashy features, and even a celebrity spokesperson.

Let China Lead

Competition between China and other nations is not a zero-sum game, where China's gains necessarily result in others' losses. If China produces more designers, scientists, and entrepreneurs than the U.S. or Europe, the world as a whole will benefit from having more of these valuable talents in its population. If China discovers a means of successfully combining capitalism and socialism, the world benefits from having a more diverse palette of effective governing options. If China challenges other developed countries' leadership in the innovation of mass transit, water purification, or environmental protection, perhaps everyone will become more motivated and resourceful in pursuing these goals.

The presence of another major world economy, particularly one that offers an alternative approaches to prosperity and whose population embraces different philosophies and adopts different behaviors, can only enrich the world. Seeing China rise to a position of leadership led by a young, entrepreneurial generation unafraid of the future, is not something to fear—it's something to envision and promote.

Photograph & Illustration Credits

Cynthia Chan: pages 6, 9 (bottom), 28, 37, 49 (bottom right), 59 (bottom right), 60, 61, 65, 73, 77, 79, 80, 82 (bottom), 86, 92, 94, 95, 96, 108, 114 (bottom), 118, 121 (top two and bottom right), 123.

Rodrigo Castillo: pages 78, 110.

Terri Ducay: pages 9 (top), 69 (top).

Etienne Fang: pages 12, 46 and 102.

Christopher Ireland: pages 10, 12, 14, 15, 19, 21, 22, 25, 27, 33, 35 (top), 36, 38, 40, 42, 44, 45, 49 (top two), 50, 52, 57, 59 (top left), 64, 66, 68 (bottom), 74 (bottom), 76 (top two and bottom right), 79, 93, 98, 106, 107, 115, 116.

David T. Lee: calligraphy pages 56, 72, 90, 112.

Katherine Lee: cover and pages 5, 34, 43, 54, 59 (top right), 68 (top), 69 (bottom), 83, 84, 87 (top), 114 (top), 119, 121 (bottom left).

Raphael Pau: calligraphy pages 29, 58, 74 (top).

Gillian Qi: page 101 (top).

Tony Senna: page 49 (bottom left).

Tathei Wong: page 88.

LiAnne Yu: pages 26, 39, 58, 59 (bottom left), 62, 70, 76 (bottom left), 81, 82 (top), 87 (bottom two).

IndexStock: page 3.

Index